D1626118

Lillian Beckwith's Hebridean Cookbook

Lillian Beckwith's Hebridean Cookbook

Illustrated by Douglas Hall

Hutchinson of London

By the same author

The Hebridean books

THE HILLS IS LONELY
THE SEA FOR BREAKFAST
THE LOUD HALO
A ROPE — IN CASE
LIGHTLY POACHED
BEAUTIFUL JUST!

Fiction

GREEN HAND
THE SPUDDY

Autobiography

ABOUT MY FATHER'S BUSINESS

Hutchinson & Co (Publishers) Ltd
3 Fitzroy Square, London W1

London Melbourne Sydney Auckland
Wellington Johannesburg and agencies
throughout the world

First published 1976
Text © Lillian Beckwith 1976
Illustrations © Hutchinson & Co (Publishers) Ltd 1976

Set in Monotype Baskerville

Printed in Great Britain by
The Anchor Press Ltd and bound by
Wm Brendon & Son Ltd
both of Tiptree, Essex

ISBN 0 09 127880 3

To 'Muffet'

In gratitude for her friendship
and co-operation throughout the
years.

Introduction

In Bruach it was necessary to bake frequently. Bread was available only once a week (weather permitting) and having already endured the land and sea journey from Glasgow invariably, by the time it reached us, it was both stale and damp, with the result that after a day, or at the most two days, it had usually sprouted such an impressive mould growth that it was fit only for feeding to the hens. Cake was unobtainable locally: to buy it one would have had to make the journey to the mainland, and though admittedly we could get biscuits from the weekly grocery van the only variety ever on sale was 'Abernethy', which for assuaging one's sweet tooth were about as effective as dry toast.

Naturally while I lived in Bruach I learned to bake the traditional Hebridean fare, which, though delicious, is of the simplest kind and limited to girdle-baked scones, bannocks and oatcakes, with perhaps a boiled fruit dumpling whenever the occasion warranted, i.e. New Year, church Communion or the visit of a seldom-seen relative from the city. I found the dumplings easy enough to make, but though it sounds and looks simple when explained or demonstrated the method of making girdle scones seems to depend on an inherited technique which, despite repeated tuition, I was unable to acquire, though my scones do make acceptable substitutes for the real thing. When girdle scones are good they are really good (though they should be eaten fresh) and I have included several recipes for them in this book, but if you do not possess a heavy girdle (or griddle, as it is called in some parts of the country) then I advise you not to bother with them. The base of a modern frying pan, which is sometimes recommended as a makeshift girdle, is not nearly thick enough to spread the heat satisfactorily and one tends to get a sticky-textured, scorched scone instead of the smooth feather-light, tawny-complexioned scone which comes off a real Hebridean girdle.

Just as I was interested in Hebridean cookery, so were the Bruachites interested in my efforts. They knew that when storms confined me to the cottage for a good part of the day they could be reasonably sure of finding me at my stove and since no one else wanted to work outside on such days my kitchen was a popular place for the 'time-passers', 'work-dodgers', or plain 'droppers-in' who liked to sit and talk to me and to one another while they watched the unfamiliar (to most of them) sights of butter and sugar being beaten to a cream; of egg whites being whisked to a stiffness that would bear an egg; of icing being piped on to a cake. Even the slicing of potatoes to form a crust for a simple hot-pot guaranteed their full attention. Such preparations sometimes brought interesting comments: 'My, but you English are the great ones for the frills,' was one observation as I shredded a cabbage prior to cooking it, and 'God! What like of beast is that you have?' was another as I took a stuffed vegetable marrow out of the oven.

Interested though they might be, however, they rarely accepted my invitations to, in their own idiom, 'stay and take a plate of dinner'. They were suspicious of what they re-

8

garded as my 'fancy' food, preferring their mutton or fish or venison or poultry to be plain-boiled in a pan with or without vegetables and with boiled potatoes squeezed straight out of their jackets on to their plates. Perhaps it sounds dull, tasteless fare, but one must remember that their food was the produce of the land and sea around them – Highland fresh and Highland flavoured. Could one ask for more? My own 'messing about' with food intrigued but did not tempt them.

It was a completely different matter when I did a batch of baking, for then they liked to sample and comment on the buns and cakes as they came out of the oven and indeed I was glad of their presence, for though croft work and the Hebridean climate had so keened my appetite that I found myself thinking constantly of food and baking had become not just a necessary habit but an enslaving hobby to be indulged in whenever there was an excuse to remain indoors, there were many times when I got so carried away trying out new recipes and adapting old ones that my output far exceeded my possible intake. I was glad too of the children who visited me, perhaps bringing a jug of milk or a pat of home-made butter from their mother, and the compliment to my cooking which I have most cherished over the years came from two lisping little tots who, while they munched chocolate cake in my kitchen, were playing a game of 'bestest in the world'. The 'bestest' woman in the world was, of course, their mother; the 'bestest' man was their father, but when they came to naming the 'bestest' place in the world they both agreed without hesitation that it was 'Lillum's kitchen'.

It saddens me to know that nowadays many children do not know the joy of returning home to a warm, spicy-smelling kitchen where Mother is perhaps hastily buttering a scone or cutting a slice of home-made cake 'to see you on until I have your tea ready'; a home where they know that when tea-time comes they will be sitting down at a simply laid table and confronted by a tasty meal that has not come out of a tin or a packet. And husbands, too, I feel sorry for in these days of convenience foods. What man is not happier for coming home to the good smell of his dinner cooking?

I was in a small grocer's shop recently when a young

woman (who had no other job than looking after her modern house and her one child) rushed in and announced she hadn't anything for 'his' dinner. Asking the shopkeeper for suggestions, she leaned over the deep-freeze cabinet with as much familiarity as she might have leaned over her child's cot.

'Chicken breast?' offered the shopkeeper.

'No, I gave him that yesterday.'

'Steak-and-kidney pudding?'

The woman giggled. 'No, I gave him that the day before.'

The shopkeeper hazarded further suggestions, but all of them were rejected with a 'No, he's had that once this week already. He might complain if I give him the same thing too often.'

In the time it had taken her to get to the shop and to select from the deep freeze I estimated she could have been well on the way with preparation for giving 'him' a cheaper and tastier meal, but it seemed the freezer cabinet at the grocer's had taken the place of her own larder and she had forgotten there was such a thing as fresh food. The woman went away eventually with a packet of frozen hamburgers, a packet of frozen vegetables, a tin of instant potato, a frozen fruit pie, and a tin of ready-made custard. If it is true that the way to a man's heart is through his stomach, then nowadays it must be equally true that the only way to a man's stomach is through an ice-cap. I wondered why a man should bother to come home regularly to such fare as 'he' apparently did, but perhaps he had an appetite as big as that of the old roadsweeper who once told me if his wife asked him what he fancied for his meal he used to tell her, 'I don't care what you give me, woman, but I'm warning you I'm that hungry just be sure when you put my plate in front of me you take your hands away quickly in case I eat them as well.'

I suppose my being for so long accustomed to the good 'Highland freshness and flavour' of food accounts for my dislike of convenience foods (though even I am willing to concede their usefulness on occasion) and my dislike has no doubt engendered also an aversion to modern kitchens, for I confess the streamlined kitchens depicted in the glossy magazines have about as much attraction for me as has an operating theatre. I like a kitchen to be functional, of course, with a sink unit and lots of easily accessible cupboards; contemporary lighting and a modern cooker, but having all that I need to compromise. My kitchen has chairs (not backless stools or benches) for the comfort of the cook and for the occasional 'droppers-in' and it has a sturdy wooden table on whose non-plastic top the privileged young can sit and swing their legs while they sample and pronounce upon the latest batch of baking. It is a place where for much of the year full wine or beer jars froth and bubble near the continuously burning cooker; where the kettle sits on the hob always halfway to being ready to provide a cup of tea or coffee; where my cooking utensils, instead of being shut away in drawers, are on display, helping to give me inspiration. 'Ah, yes,' I think, as my eye lights upon the steak hammer, 'maybe banana steak for supper tonight.' Or perhaps seeing the parsley cutter I might have a fancy for plain boiled bacon with parsley sauce. There is a folksy touch in the row of willow-patterned meat dishes (bought years ago at a junk shop for half a crown the lot) which are ranged along the highest of the open shelves and since willow pattern possesses the property of looking clean even when it isn't it is only I who know that the height of the shelf discourages me from taking down the dishes to wash them more than twice a year and that when I do I am ashamed of the subsequent colour of the water. Without a qualm of conscience I swallow the complimentary remarks of visitors about the fresh and decorative look the dishes give to the kitchen.

However, my kitchen is not so folksy as to have acquired such sought-after antiques as a Victorian oil lamp (though a genuine hurricane lamp does hang discreetly in a corner ready for emergencies), a rocking chair or a peg rug. These days Victorian oil lamps flaunt themselves at front windows, and peg rugs, having been dismissed as unhygienic, are no longer obtainable. Hygiene apart, I have never found a modern rug that is half so cosy and at the same time so hard-wearing as the old peg rugs on which, as a child, I used to sit or lie in front of the open range. And, except for being taken up for their daily shaking, peg rugs have the advantage of staying complacently in position whereas modern rugs are flibbertygibbets in comparison, inclined to roll at the corners and catch an unwary toe or else skid across the floor at the slightest stumble. So my kitchen has no rug at present. Only an uncluttered wipe-clean floor which will do until (and then hygiene be blowed) I can get around to making myself a good old-fashioned peg rug.

Having now introduced you to my kitchen and inflicted upon you some of my likes and dislikes, let me now confess that I am no 'cordon bleu' cook, nor have I ever had any aspirations in that direction. But I love cooking and as my young friends say, in the modern idiom, I can produce some 'gorgeous nosh'. Here then is my collection, a hotch-potch of 'receipts' handed down from my own and other people's grandmothers; recipes from old cookery books; improvisations and use-ups and as such I offer them to you. They range from what might be termed 'survival' recipes through the frankly economical to what these days might be looked upon as extravagant, but they are all tasty and fairly easy to cook. My use of seasoning may not always be to your liking, but seasoning is such a matter of personal taste that I suggest you do the same as I do – sample as you cook.

There is an old Manx saying which goes: 'When one poor man sets out to help another poor man God Himself laughs.' I do not think I could be fairly described as a 'poor cook', but all the same I hope God doesn't have too good a laugh at our expense.

Oven temperatures

Slow oven	275 to 325 degrees F.
Moderate oven	325 to 375 ,,
Moderately hot oven	375 to 425 ,,
Hot oven	425 to 475 ,,
Very hot oven	475 to 500 ,,

Girdle temperatures

When I asked my Bruach neighbours how I could tell when the girdle was hot enough for baking the various scones and pancakes they replied that one must learn to know the smell of the heat. The knowledge soon comes, but until you have acquired it here is a rough guide.

Sprinkle a little flour on the girdle. Leave it for a minute and then stir with a knife blade. If it shows signs of becoming pale brown it is the right heat for pancakes. For oatcakes the flour should take two minutes to become pale brown and for scones nearer three minutes.

Unless otherwise stated, plain flour is used in all the recipes.

A 5 ml spoon is the equivalent of 1 teaspoon.
A 15 ml spoon is the equivalent of 1 tablespoon.

13

Contents of Recipes

Poultry

Chicken with almonds; Chicken cream; Chicken and lemon pie;
Chicken Maryland, with corn fritters; Chicken pie; Coq au vin

Game

Cormorant casserole; Grouse, roast; Rabbit; Rabbit, roast whole;
Rabbit curry; Rabbit pie; Rabbit fricasse; Rabbit hotpot; Rabbit,
fried; Venison; Venison, roast haunch; Venison chops; Venison stew

Savoury Dishes 97

Bacon, egg and cheese pie; Bacon, onion and potato hotpot;
Bacon and onion roly poly; Birdy pancakes; Black pudding; Blaven
roll; Bubble and squeak; Cauliflower au gratin; Cheese balls;
Cheese omelette; Cheese and onion batter; Cheese pudding; Cream
and bacon flan; Cuillin potatoes; Curried eggs; Egg cocottes;
Egg puffs; Haggis (mock); Harvest sausage; Kyle sausage hotpot;
Macaroni cheese; Meat and potato wads; Mushroom scramble;
Oatmeal, cheese and tomato pie; Onions au gratin; Onion, stuffed
and baked; Potato boulettes; Quick pizza; Rhuna hash; Risotto;
Sausage casserole; Sausage and tomato pie; Savoury sausage flan;
Scottish mealy pudding; Skirlie; Swedes au gratin; Tomato bacon
toast

Puddings and Sweets

Apple cheesey; Apple crumble; Apple flan; Apple pancakes;
Apple pie; Apple snow; Ballyre fudge pudding; Banana pudding;
Banana supreme; Bread-and-butter pudding; Bruach cloth dumpling;
Carrageen mould; Cherry and almond crumble; Chocolat au rhum;
Christmas pudding; Comfrey-leaf pancakes; Elderflower dips;
Cottage pudding; Daffodil pudding; Elderberry sponge; Fig pudding;
French tart; Ginger-nut pudding; Lemon cream without cream;
Lemon-meringue pie; Lemon mousse; Lemon snow; Marsala custard;
Peach cream; Peach delight; Pears with chocolate sauce; Pineapple
soufflé; Pineapple upside-down pudding; Prune soufflé; Queen
pudding; Star Queen pudding; Scottish black bun; Spotted Dick;
Strawberry meringue tart; Strawberry shortcake; Syrup sponge
pudding; Syrup tart; Zebra pudding

Bread 145

Irish wholemeal loaf; Steam bread (without yeast); Wholewheat
bread; Wholewheat splits

Cakes, Large and Small, Buns and Biscuits 153

Apricot cakes; Banana bunloaf; Barm brack; Broken biscuit slices;
Bruach winter cake; Caramel sponge sandwich; Ceilidh shortbread;
Chocolate éclairs; Cinnamon cookies; Cream horns; Curly cookies;
Date and mincemeat slice; Ginger cookies; Granny's bunloaf;
Hazelnut bunloaf; Iced fruit slices; Irish brack; Marmalade teabread;
Morag's teabread; Mother's Johnny cake; Old-fashioned ginger-
bread; Orange buns; Quick coconut pyramids; Sorrel slices;
Sheehan cakes; Strawberry cake; Strupak biscuits; Teacakes;
Undressed bride's cake; Waffles; Walnut biscuits

Scones 175

Barley-meal scones; Bruach girdle scones; Bruach oatcakes; Bruach
potato scones; Bruach scads; Cheese scones; Drop scones (or Scotch
pancakes); Flapjack; Fruit scones; Oatmeal bannocks; Potato
scones, thick; Sultana pancakes; Wholemeal scones

Sauces 185

Savoury

Apple sauce; Bechamel sauce; Caper sauce; Cockle sauce;
Hollandaise sauce; Mock Hollandaise sauce; Mushroom sauce;
Onion sauce; Parsley sauce; Pork special sauce; Sauce Robert;
Shrimp sauce; Tomato sauce; White sauce

Sweet

Brandy butter (1 & 2); Brandy sauce; Butterscotch sauce; Caramel
brandy sauce; Chocolate sauce with syrup; Marmalade
orange sauce

Miscellaneous 195

Burying for preservation; Hawthorn jelly; Rhubarb and loganberry
jam; Rowan and apple jelly; Eldeberry wine; Heather ale;
Mock whisky; Nettle beer; Rose brandy; Sherry wine; Vine
prunings wine; Porridge; Biscuit pastry; Garlic bread; Garlic
cabbage; Madeira grapefruit; Onion badjis; Savoury pies (to eat
with roast mutton)

Asthma cure 1; Asthma cure 2; Cough medicine; Cough cure
(drastic); Rough cider cold cure; Drawing ointment; Hair tonic;
Plantain poultice; Rose tonic; Stomach ulcers, cure for; Sore-throat
cure; Temperature, to bring down; Warts, cures for; Conger eel fat
(for rheumatism); Comfrey leaf tea; Puffball powder; Weak chest
cure

Soups

Except for lobster bisque my soups are all 'gut warmers', thick, and satisfying. Consommés I regard as invalid fare. Here are all my favourites; I am sorry they do not include Scotch broth.

Chicken-and-carrot Soup

Chicken remains (bones, skin, etc.)	1 oz (25 gm) butter
2 pints (1¼ litres) water	1 tablespn flour
2 med. sized onions	Salt and pepper
1 small turnip (about ¼ lb or 100 gm)	Bouquet garni
	1 lb (450 gm) carrots
1 stalk celery	1 tablespn chopped parsley

Simmer the remains of the chicken in the water for about two hours, then put through a coarse sieve. Peel and chop the onions finely; grate the celery and the turnip. Fry the onions, celery and turnip in the butter until pale brown; stir in the flour, add the chicken stock, seasoning and the bouquet garni. Simmer for ten minutes. Meanwhile grate the carrot and add to the soup. Taste for seasoning and continue to simmer for another ten minutes. Remove the bouquet garni and sprinkle each plate of soup with parsley before serving.

Country Soup

2 oz (50 gm) butter or bacon fat	1 stalk celery
2 med. sized potatoes	1 tablespn tomato purée
2 large onions	2 pints (1¼ litres) stock
1 small turnip	1 teaspn cornflour
3 med. sized carrots	Bouquet garni

Chop the onions and fry in the fat until transparent. Either chop or mince the potatoes, turnip, carrot, and celery. Put

21

into the pan with the onion and fry for one minute. Add the tomato purée, stir in the cornflour and add the stock and bouquet garni. Simmer for thirty minutes with the lid on. Remove bouquet garni. Serve garnished with chopped parsley and fried croutons (I always add any cold left-over vegetables to this soup).

Curry Soup

1 large onion	1 pint (600 ml) stock (made
1 oz (25 gm) butter	with beef cube if necessary)
1 dessertspn (10 ml) tomato purée	Salt and pepper
1 teaspn cornflour	1 bayleaf
1 teaspn curry paste	Squeeze of lemon juice

Chop the onion and fry gently in the butter until golden brown. Add tomato purée to the pan. Stir in the cornflour, curry paste and then the stock. Bring to the boil, stirring well. Add the salt and pepper, the lemon juice and the bayleaf. Simmer for ten minutes. Remove the bayleaf and serve with croutons.

A dessertspoonful (25 gm) of long grain rice may be added to the soup after the seasonings have been added. The soup should then be simmered for twenty minutes instead of ten minutes.

Dulse Soup

1 lb (450 gm) fresh dulse (weight	3 oz (75 gm) oatmeal
when wet)	Seasoning
2 pints (1¼ litres) water	

Rinse the fresh dulse well and put into a pan with the cold water. Bring to the boil and simmer for one hour. Strain and re-boil. Mix the oatmeal with enough cold water to make a thin creamy consistency, stir it carefully into the soup and continue to boil for a further ten minutes. Season to taste.

Do not throw away the boiled dulse but mix it with raw oatmeal and pepper and salt if needed and use as a vegetable.

Dulse is one of our commonest seaweeds and grows abundantly on tide-washed rocks around the shore. It is dark red in colour and its leaves (or 'fronds' as they are more correctly called) fan out from the root and lie flat against the rocks like strips of sodden paper. They are about four inches long and about half an inch wide.

Green Pea Soup

'Peas are so nourishing that only water, not stock, is needed to make pea soup.' So says an old recipe book of my mother's. It also adds: 'A peck of young peas will not yield more than enough for one meal for a couple of hearty pea-eaters unless the pods be very full when there may be enough for three.'

According to my information a peck is the equivalent of two gallons and since I reckon a quart of shelled peas is roughly a pound in weight it seems to imply that a 'hearty pea-eater' will consume four pounds of peas at a sitting! Even if the writer is referring to peas in their pods, allowing for two pounds of pods to yield one pound of peas, it still allows the pea-eater two pounds as his portion. Confronted with such a glut of peas I should make pea soup.

2 lb (900 gm) peas (in their pods)	Parsley
1 lettuce	3 oz (75 gm) butter
1 slice lean bacon or ham	1 oz (25 gm) cornflour
10 leaves spinach	1 lump sugar
1 onion	1 quart (1¼ litres) water
1 sprig mint	Salt and pepper

Pod the peas and boil the pods for at least half an hour. Strain. Wash the spinach and lettuce and shred it. Slice the onion and chop the bacon. Melt the butter in a saucepan and add the bacon, peas, lettuce, onion, spinach, mint, salt and pepper and let them cook very gently, stirring occasionally to prevent burning. When vegetables are quite soft put them through a sieve. Return the pulp to the pan and add the water in which the pods have been boiled – make up to one quart (1¼ litres) and add the lump of sugar. Mix the corn-flour with a little water to a smooth paste and add to the pan. Test for seasoning. Bring to the boil and simmer for ten minutes. Sprinkle with chopped parsley before serving.

Ham-bone Soup

Ham bones
Approx. 2 quarts 2½ (litres) water
3 med. sized carrots
1 lb (450 gm) turnip

1 large onion
6 oz (175 gm) lentils
(Any left-over vegetables)

Put the ham bones and water in a pan and bring to the boil. Finely chop half of the carrots and half of the turnip and the whole of the onion. Grate the remaining carrot and turnip and add all the vegetables and lentils to the soup. Bring back to the boil. Simmer for one hour. Bring to a quick boil ten minutes before serving.

Lobster Bisque (Economical)

Lobster shell
Salt and pepper
Pinch sweet basil
1 oz (25 gm) butter

1 tablespn flour
2 pints (1¼ litres) water
¼ pint (150 ml) cream

Pound the lobster shell into small pieces and put into the cold water along with the salt and pepper and sweet basil. Bring to the boil and simmer for one and a half to two hours. Sieve the liquid carefully so that no pieces of shell remain.

Meanwhile melt the butter in a saucepan. Stir in the flour until it begins to froth. Add lobster stock slowly, stirring continuously. Cook for ten minutes. Remove from heat and stir in the fresh cream.

If you want to be more extravagant you can, of course, add flaked lobster flesh to the bisque.

Onion Soup

2 large onions
1 oz (25 gm) butter
1 pint (600 ml) beef-cube stock
1 oz (25 gm) grated cheese

1 teaspn chopped parsley
Pepper and salt
2 level teaspns flour

Chop onion finely and cook in butter until golden brown. Stir in two teaspoons of flour. Add stock slowly. Season and simmer for about fifteen minutes until onions are tender. Serve with grated cheese and parsley sprinkled on top.

A minced hard-boiled egg added to any of these soups about five minutes before it has finished cooking is a good thickener.

Also I sometimes use potato flour instead of cornflour. You can use instant potato to thicken soups, of course, but then you should follow the instructions on the tin as to when to add it.

Tomato Soup

1 med. sized onion	1 teaspn cornflour
1 oz (25 gm) butter	1 can tomato juice
1 slice lean bacon, chopped	Pinch mixed herbs
½ teaspn sugar	½ cup (50 ml) water or milk

Chop and fry onion in butter until just beginning to brown. Add the bacon and fry for one minute. Stir in tomato juice, sugar and mixed herbs, and cornflour mixed with half a cup of water or milk, and simmer for five minutes. I like to eat this soup with the 'bits' left in, but some people prefer it sieved.

Shellfish

Nowadays shellfish bought from the shops is invariably already boiled but I give the instructions for cooking in case the day comes when you are able or perhaps compelled to help yourselves to the treasures of the sea.

It is essential not to overcook shellfish. Overcooking makes them tough and leathery – like plastic buttons that have been too long in the wash.

Always remember that all shellfish (including the humble winkle) can be mixed with a cheese or white sauce and put into vol-au-vent cases to make delicious cocktail savouries.

Remember too that the shells of lobster, prawns and scampi boiled in water for an hour or two will give a good stock for bisques or fish soups.

Crabs

In Bruach crab roasting was indulged in as companionably as the English custom of chestnut roasting except that crabs were available all the year round. Indeed they were so plentiful that we used to take off only the two big claws and discard all the rest. The claws were pushed into the ashes of the peat fire for about ten minutes and then cracked open with a poker, the flesh being pulled out with the fingers where that was possible while the less accessible flesh was sucked out.

This method is not only wasteful but some of the tastiest flesh is in the shell of the crab.

I prefer crab served plain with a green salad, but there were occasions when I had a fancy for a 'Crab scramble'. But first let us talk about the preparation of the crab.

Assuming you have bought a live crab, drop it into a pan of boiling water, re-boil, and simmer for ten to twenty minutes (no longer) according to size. Take the pan off the heat and leave the crab to cool in the water. A medium-sized crab is usually the best value.

If you have purchased a crab which is already cooked you should try shaking it gently first; a sloshy sound indicates that there's more water than flesh inside it. Good crabs feel heavy for their size.

Turn the cooked crab on its back and pull off all the claws. With a toffee hammer or similar tool tap along the dark line that runs round the underside about half an inch from the edge of the shell. Now, holding the back shell firmly in one hand and the body part in the other, pull apart. Remove the stomach bag (which is like a tiny plastic bag and lies just underneath the head part of the shell) and also take out any intestine (this is like a thin grey or black thread) which is attached to the stomach. Make sure you throw these away. Scrape out all the meat remaining in the shell; this includes the brown meat (sometimes greeny brown) and the soft pinky flesh, which is fat and rich. Put the flesh into a basin. Wash and dry the shell. Take the body of the crab and pull off what are usually called the 'dead men's fingers', which are greyish frond-like pieces and are inedible. Pick out the flesh from the body and add it to the flesh in the basin. Now crack the claws (you might need a more substantial hammer for this) and take out the flesh, using a skewer to reach the flesh in the tiny crevices. Flake the claw meat and mix with the rest of the meat, season to taste with salt and pepper and per-haps a dash of vinegar or salad cream if you must. Pile back into the shell and decorate with chopped parsley. Serve with green salad.

Crab Scramble

2 oz (50 gm) butter	2 tablespn milk
4 eggs	Small pinch celery salt or
Flaked crab meat	ordinary salt
1 teaspn curry powder	Black pepper

Beat the eggs with the milk. Melt butter, stir in curry powder and crab meat. When thoroughly hot stir in the eggs and milk. Add seasonings. Cook quickly, stirring continuously, until thick. Serve on hot buttered toast.

When I was a child in Cheshire the truculent old cockle man used to come round with his horse and cart, flaying the town with his bellowing cry of 'Cock . . . les . . . er, cock . . . les . . . er', and my father, calling to Mother to look after the shop while he was out, would take off his white apron and jacket and hurry off to catch the cockle-cart to buy a pint or half-pint of cockles. My mother refused to go and buy cockles for him, partly because she was revolted by the sight of any sort of shellfish and partly because, like most of the other women in the district, she was too sensitive to go within range of the cockleman's blasphemous tongue. Father had not only to buy his own cockles but he also had to prepare them himself, which he must have done successfully since I recall seeing him with a tumblerful of cockles steeped in spice and vinegar and eating with great relish.

Not even in times of scarcity in Bruach did I manage to cultivate a taste for cockles. I gathered some once and boiled and tasted them, but I found them gritty and tough and much less palatable than winkles. I was told by an old cockle-gatherer to whom I confided my dislike of cockles that I had done wrong to boil them. In his own words, this is how I should have gone about preparing and eating them.

'Gather your cockles and open them in the way the Lord intended them to be opened. Take a cockle in each hand and lock the hinged parts of the joints together. Press and give a sharp twist and one, if not both, of the cockles will open up. All you will need to do then is to swill them in the good clean sea and swallow them fresh.'

I confess I have never tried them this way. The only way I like cockles is in a sauce (page 188).

Lobster

As with crab I think lobster is best served plain with salad.

The cooking instructions for lobster are much the same as those for crab although purists say you should put the live lobster into cold water and bring to the boil since they keep their colour better. That way is not for me. Allow roughly ten minutes for a small lobster to twenty minutes for a large one, taking the time from when the water re-boils after immersion of the lobster.

When cool, pull off the claws and legs. Twist the tail off from where it joins the body and with a knife or pair of scissors cut up the underside of the tail, bend it open and pull out the tail flesh. Break the two breast flaps off the body part and scrape out any pink fat adhering to them. Pull the back away from the part where the legs were attached. Now find the stomach bag which like that of the crab resembles a small plastic bag and lies just below the lobster's 'chin', and discard it along with any thin dark intestinal thread adhering to it. This thread also runs through the centre of the tail flesh as you would expect, so gently prise apart the flesh and remove the thread. Also discard the 'dead men's fingers' that adhere to the part that carries the legs – in fact discard any tough membraneous parts you find; the rest is edible. Pick the flesh off this part and add to the rest. Scrape out the tail shell and the back shell to get the pink fat, if there is any. Crack the large claws and remove the flesh from them and if you have a skewer and lots of patience (or a willing family) similarly pick out the flesh from the legs. I just put them in a dish and leave them for people to suck.

Flake or roughly pull apart the white flesh and mix it with the pink and red fat. Serve with salad. Lobster is also very good mixed with a mock hollandaise sauce or with mayonnaise and piled into a large or several small vol-au-vent cases.

Lobster Omelette

1 boiled lobster, about 1 lb (450 gm) in weight	Pepper and salt
	2 oz (50 gm) butter
4 eggs	Parsley for garnish

Remove the flesh from the lobster and put it through a mincer. Whisk up four eggs and season them with pepper and salt. Add the lobster flesh and whisk again thoroughly.

Melt the butter in an omelette pan and when hot pour in the mixture. Put over moderate heat, stirring one way until the omelette is set. Fold it over and turn on to a hot dish. Garnish with parsley and serve at once.

Mussels

These are in season only when there is an R in the month. They must be alive when bought, i.e. their shells must be tight shut. Never and I repeat never buy mussels whose shells gape even an eighth of an inch unless when you tap the shell sharply it snaps shut immediately.

1 pint (600 ml) mussels
2 oz (50 gm) butter
2 tablespn flour
Approx. ¼ pint (150 ml) milk
Pepper
Salt if necessary

Pinch celery salt
Pinch sweet basil
1 teaspn lemon juice
Chopped parsley
1 bayleaf

Wash and scrub the mussels thoroughly in several changes of water so as to remove any trace of sand. Put into a large shallow pan which has a tight-fitting lid one bayleaf and then the mussels with only the water adhering to their shells. Put on the lid and shake the pan over gentle heat until the mussels have opened their shells. Drain off the liquid into a basin. With a pair of scissors remove the little black beard (like a tiny tuft of seaweed) from each mussel. Remove the mussels from their shells.

Heat butter in a saucepan; stir in two tablespoons of flour; add the liquid from the fish and make up to half a pint (300 ml) with the milk. Season with pepper and a pinch of celery salt, adding other salt only if necessary. Add the sweet basil and the lemon juice. Bring to the boil and simmer for one minute. Add chopped parsley and finally add the mussels. Heat until the sauce just begins to come to the boil and then serve with hot buttered toast.

Prawns bought in shops are already boiled but if you have to deal with freshly caught prawns drop them into boiling water and boil for two minutes.

Since I am somewhat fastidious about shellfish when I prepare prawns I always look for and discard any dark intestinal thread that runs through the tail but it is such an irksome process that I doubt if chefs take the trouble. But don't worry – prawns too are fastidious.

Prawn Cocktail

1 lb (450 gm) prawns	Slices of tomato
Pepper	Paprika pepper
Mayonnaise	Lettuce leaves, from the heart

Shell the prawns and dust lightly with pepper. Mix with mayonnaise or salad cream. Line some hors-d'œuvre glasses with the lettuce leaves (well dried) and fill them with the prawn and mayonnaise mixture. Decorate with slices of tomato cut into quarters and finish with a tiny shake of paprika pepper. Chill before serving.

If you boil up the prawn shells in about a quart ($1\frac{1}{4}$ litres) of water for an hour or so you can use the liquid either for strengthening the flavour of the lobster bisque (page 24) or make a prawn bisque using the same recipe.

Curried Prawns

1 lb (450 gm) prawns in shell	1 teaspn tomato purée (optional)
2 med. sized onions	1 teaspn brown sugar
1 teaspn curry powder – more if you like hot curry	$\frac{1}{3}$ pint (175 ml) of stock made from prawn shells
$\frac{1}{2}$ teaspn curry paste	Salt, cayenne pepper
1 oz (25 gm) butter	2 teaspn lemon juice
1 dessertspn flour	1 tablespn chutney

First shell the prawns and boil up the shells in a pint of water.

Peel and chop the onions finely. Melt the butter and fry

the onions until golden brown; add the curry powder and paste and the flour. Cook for five minutes; add the tomato purée if used and sugar and then the prawn-shell stock. Bring to the boil. Add the salt and cayenne pepper, lemon juice and the chutney. Simmer for thirty minutes. Add the shelled prawns, cooking gently for about six minutes. Serve with boiled rice.

Prawn Fritters

Quarter pint (150 ml) prawns (after shelling)	2 tablespn water
2 oz (50 gm) flour	1 egg white
1 dessertspn salad oil	Deep fat for frying
	Salt and pepper

Sieve the flour and seasoning. Make a well in the centre; stir in the oil and just enough water to make a thick coating batter. Fold in the stiffly beaten egg white. Dip the prawns into the batter and drop into smoking hot fat. Fry until crisp and golden brown. Drain and serve.

Scallops

These are delicious but when buying them make sure the flesh is creamy white and the roe a bright orange colour. Grey-tinged or yellowy flesh shows that they are not fresh. Scallops are not cooked before being sold but they have usually been taken from their shells. If buying them in their shells you can open them by inserting the point of a knife into the muscle at the hinge of the shell. Carefully remove the scallop, cutting off the beard and any black part. Wash them very thoroughly to remove sand.

They are rich and very filling and half a pound of shelled scallops is ample for two people. While there are more elaborate ways of cooking them I find this the easiest and the tastiest.

½ lb (225 gm) of scallops	Salt and pepper
2 oz (50 gm) butter	Milk
2 tablespn flour	Pinch of sweet basil
¼ teaspn lemon juice	

Heat the butter in a pan, making it hot but not smoking hot. Dry the scallops in kitchen paper and toss them in the seasoned flour. Stir them gently into the fat and cook for about three minutes. Add a pinch of sweet basil and just enough milk or milk and water to make a thickish sauce. Add the lemon juice and serve with thin bread and butter.

Queenies

These are like baby scallops and have no orange roe but they are even more delicately flavoured. They should be cooked as above but only for two minutes instead of three. Both queenies and scallops can be cooked in the batter as for prawns (see page 33).

Scampi

The recipe for prawn fritters can also be used for scampi.

If you can get fresh scampi then it is nice just to drop them into boiling water for ten minutes – certainly no longer. Provide each guest with a tiny dish of melted butter and leave them to shell their own scampi.

If you buy ready-boiled scampi then here is a nice dish:

1 lb (450 gm) shelled scampi
2 oz (50 gm) butter
3 tablespn salad oil
1 onion, chopped finely

4 tomatoes (skinned and sliced)
12 button mushrooms
1 teaspn lemon juice
Salt pepper
Parsley

Heat the butter together with the oil in a pan. Fry the chopped onion. Add the tomatoes, mushrooms and scampi and fry for about ten minutes, stirring all the time. Season with salt and pepper. Add lemon juice. Decorate with chopped parsley.

Winkles

These are always sold boiled but if you have to deal with live winkles drop them into boiling water for not more than two minutes. When cool enough to handle, discard the 'front door' and draw out the winkle with a pin or pointed match-stick. They are best eaten whilst sitting round the fire – each person picking out his own winkles. If they are accompanied by potatoes baked in their jackets and served with lots of melted butter so much the better.

Fish

I was talking to a newly married young friend one day and she mentioned that she was on her way to the shops to buy some fish fingers for her husband's dinner.

'I love fish fingers, don't you?' she asked me.

'I've never tasted them,' I replied.

'What, never?'

I shook my head, amused at the incredulity in her voice.

'Oh, but you must have,' she insisted. 'Perhaps you had them when you were a little girl and now you've forgotten you ever had them.'

'My dear,' I told her, 'fish fingers weren't invented when I was a little girl.'

'Not invented?' She was utterly perplexed. 'But fish fingers didn't have to be invented, surely? They just are.'

'They just weren't,' I laughed. 'They've only recently come to the market. Recently by my standards,' I added. 'That means within the last fifteen years or so.' I was surprised myself at the number of years fish fingers had been available.

But my friend was only eighteen and I could see she couldn't envisage life without fish fingers. 'And haven't you wanted to taste them in all that time?' she persisted.

'Never. I happen to like my fish as it comes from the sea and before it's pulverized and patterned by machines.'

Her expression revealed that my statement had confirmed her opinion of my eccentricity. As a matter of fact I was in Hong Kong when I tasted my first fish finger and I admit I found it pleasant enough. It did betray traces of its marine environment and I have no doubt if I had been given fish fingers as a child I might have become just as addicted to them as was my young friend.

It is probably impossible to buy cods' livers so that one would need to catch one's fish and preserve the liver instead of discarding it with the entrails. But given one or two cods' livers this is the nicest possible way of taking cod-liver oil. If you can come by a cod's gullet this mixture makes a nice stuffing for it.

Cod-liver Pie

2 fresh cods' livers	¼ lb (100 gm) oatmeal
1 large onion	Salt and pepper

Quarter the onion. Drop cods' livers and onion into boiling water and boil for two minutes. Lift them out and mince. Mix with oatmeal, salt and pepper and moisten with a little of the water in which the liver and onion have been boiled only if the mixture is too dry. Remember that the oil from the livers will moisten the dish during cooking. Bake in a moderate oven for about half an hour. Since this dish is very rich it is wise to eat only a little at a time.

This is not the only way of eating cod's liver. One old Bruach fisherman told me that it was usual for the men on his boat to take some of the livers from the cod they caught and put them between two thick slices of bread. Then they would wrap the 'sandwiches' in a fold of oilskin and put them on the seat in the wheelhouse where the skipper would be sure to sit on them for a few hours. When they felt peckish they retrieved their sandwiches which of course were now impregnated with the oil squeezed from the livers.

The first time I was confronted with a conger eel was in Bruach when Erchy arrived at the house one night with the great black fish slung on his back like the man on the label of the old 'Scott's Emulsion' bottles. The conger eel was all of six foot long and at its thickest about eighteen inches in girth.

'What on earth do I do with it?' I demanded as he hung it on a hook behind the kitchen door.

'Damned if I know,' he replied. 'But you're always after sayin' you'll cook anythin' that comes out of the sea so you might just as well try your hand at this beast.'

'I'm willing to try it,' I murmured, 'but I'm not tackling it now.' It was then about nine o'clock and I had just changed from my outdoor clothes so that I could sit and read for an hour before going to bed.

Erchy surveyed the wet patch on the floor made by the conger's tail. 'God!' he exclaimed in an awed voice, 'I thought the beast would smash the boat to pieces before we got the tiller to it to kill it.' He leaned against the wall, still breathless after carrying the eel from the shore. 'There was the three us just in the boat an' not one of us could get a hold of the beast. Indeed I was wishin' I had a beard the way they used to grow them.' He stopped short as there came a hail from outside and just as I was about to ask what on earth growing a beard would have to do with controlling a conger eel. 'That's Tearlaich shoutin' for me,' he said hurriedly. 'See now an' wait till I come to cut this beast up for you in the mornin'. You can take what flesh you're wantin' an' the rest might do for bait.' He hurried off to join his crony.

Later that night I was in my bedroom holding back sleep until I could get between the bedclothes when there was a great thumping and banging on the back door accompanied by the sound of breaking crockery and the clang of metal. In Bruach one did not bother to lock one's door except perhaps as an added defence against the storms, and thumps and bangs in the night though they might cause irritation aroused no panic. They could be made by the cattle or horses fighting over sheltered places to settle down or they might come from a party of the more boisterous of the young people who thought nothing of 'dropping in' for a 'cayley' however late the hour. So, though I felt a little peevish as I reached for a torch and went downstairs I felt no apprehension; at least not until I pointed the beam of the torch towards the kitchen from which direction the noise was coming and then I stood petrified. The dead, the very dead and gutted, conger eel was thrashing and beating itself against the kitchen door as if determined to release itself from the hook on which it hung. In its struggles the eel had knocked down a basin from the shelf and smashed it while a galvanized pail lay where it had rolled after it had spilled its load of peats on the floor. My first feeling of fright was succeeded by a momentary upsurge of anger against Erchy for not having ensured the conger was properly dead before he left it with me, but its gaping belly where the guts had been torn out reproached me with its incontrovertible evidence of the impossibility of it still being alive. As I stood watching it the conger went suddenly quite still and after a moment or two I was able to reassure myself that there was nothing uncanny about the situation; that it was in fact only delayed muscular reaction. I returned to my bed but during the night I was for a second time disturbed by the writhing assault of the conger against the door but this time I was asleep again even before I could begin to ponder about the indefiniteness of death.

The following day, as he had promised, Erchy, attended by Tearlaich, called in to cut up the conger for me. I told him of the happenings in the night.

'Indeed I should have given you warnin' of that,' Erchy said with only a faint trace of apology in his tone. 'You could have got a nasty smack yourself if you'd been near it at the time.'

As he spoke I was sprinkling salt over the portion of white flesh he had taken from the eel but I drew back involuntarily as the flesh began to quiver and ripple like wind-teased grass as the salt touched it. 'It's incredible,' I breathed.

'What is?' asked Tearlaich.

I demonstrated with the salt again.

'Ach, it'll keep doin' that for days yet like enough,' he said with such indifference that I knew his statement to be wildly exaggerated.

'Erchy,' I taxed him when he and Tearlaich were enjoying a cup of tea and a scone. 'When you told me about killing the conger eel you said something about wishing you had a beard. Did I hear you right?'

'Aye, you did.'

'What did you mean by that?'

Erchy wiped his mouth with a piece of the bleached flour sack that did duty as a handkerchief or as an engine rag as the occasion required.

'I meant what I said. I was wishin' I had a beard like old

Shamus. You mind him that had the great beard nearly down to his stomach?'

'Oh yes, I remember Shamus,' I agreed.

'Aye well, you see if old Shamus was in the boat when we caught a conger he'd grab it an' push its head up right under his chin beneath his beard an' the conger would lie there still as a corpse.'

'It would lie that still he could hold it with one hand while he stroked it with the other an' talked to it,' corroborated Tearlaich.

'Talked to it?' I echoed.

'Aye, an' God knows what he said to it but somehow he'd get that eel to bring up the hook that was in it.'

'How he did it I never knew,' mused Tearlaich, 'but right enough after a wee whiley of strokin' an' talkin' to it Shamus would turn an' hand us the hook an' all the time the eel would be lyin there without so much as a twitch of its tail.'

'And then what happened?'

They both looked puzzled for an instant but then Erchy explained: 'What happened was that we could use it again to see if we could catch somethin' better than a conger eel.'

I hid a smile. 'It's not the hook I want to know about, it's the conger. What happened to the conger?'

'Ach, Shamus would just throw it back into the sea. He would never kill a conger would Shamus. All he wanted was for us to get our hook back.' Seeing my look of surprise he added: 'What would be the use of bringing it ashore? Nobody hereabouts would think of eatin' the beast.'

'What about lobster bait, or crab bait?' I asked. 'You're always complaining you're short of that.'

'Indeed neither the lobsters nor the crabs think much of it either,' Erchy said. 'Not when they can get anythin' better.'

Unlike the crabs and the lobsters I found the conger extremely palatable.

Conger Eel

I include this recipe though I imagine conger eel is not widely sold by fishmongers these days. But you never know;

you could be lucky enough to catch yourself a conger or maybe meet a fisherman who has no other use for it than to give it to you.

About 2 lb (900 gm) of the middle part of the conger

½ lb (225 gm) fresh breadcrumbs

1 onion, finely chopped

1 dessertspn chopped parsley

Pinch thyme

Pinch mace

Pepper and salt

1 oz (25 gm) flour

2 oz (50 gm) butter

1 oz (25 gm) shredded suet

1 egg yolk

Milk

¼ pint (150 ml) water (approx.)

Fillet the conger and open it out flat on a board. Mix the breadcrumbs, parsley, onion, thyme, mace, pepper, salt and suet together. Add the egg yolk and also a little milk to make the stuffing nicely moist. Spread the stuffing on the conger and roll up. Tie with tape or string. Put into a casserole with the water. Dredge the conger with flour and spread the top with little shavings of butter. Put the lid on the casserole and bake in a moderately hot oven for about an hour. Remove the lid of the casserole. Baste the eel well with the liquid and return to the oven for a further ten to fifteen minutes.

Dog Fish

Since I understand that dog fish are sometimes sold as 'rock salmon' perhaps they would sound more appetizing if I referred to them as such. But 'rock salmon' sounds to me to be far too refined a name for these voracious fish which resemble miniature sharks and which have skins so rough that even the sea-calloused hands of professional fishermen have to be protected from them by strong gloves. They abound in the sea, will take virtually any bait and when caught have a persecuted look as if they had always known they had been born to suffer man's contempt and hostility. They are usually skinned before they are landed from the boats and appear to keep fresh for a longer period than most other fish.

They can be chopped into steaks, dipped in batter and fried, or they can be boiled in water to which a bayleaf has been added (ten minutes for a pound of fish) and served with parsley sauce. However, I prefer this fish made into a pie:

Dog Fish (or Rock Salmon) Pie

2 oz (50 gm) butter	$\frac{1}{4}$ teaspn mustard
1 lb (450 gm) fish, boiled for ten minutes and flaked	1 tablespn parsley, chopped
	3 oz (75 gm) grated cheese
1 onion, chopped	1 dessertspn mushroom ketchup
1 tablespoon flour	Brown breadcrumbs
$\frac{1}{2}$ pint (300 ml) of milk	Mashed potatoes, approx. 1 lb
Salt and pepper	(450 gm) when cooked

Melt half the butter in a saucepan and fry the onion until transparent. Stir in the flour and mustard and add the milk slowly, stirring as it comes to the boil. Beat until smooth. Add the salt and pepper, the chopped parsley, the cheese and the mushroom ketchup. Add the fish. Put into a fireproof dish. Top with a layer of mashed potato. Sprinkle with breadcrumbs: dot with remaining butter. Bake for ten minutes in a moderate oven.

Finnan Haddock

1 fillet of fish per person	1 teaspn chopped parsley
2 oz (50 gm) of butter, or more if liked	Pepper

Lay the fillets in a well-buttered grill pan and brush the top of each fillet well with melted butter. Dust with pepper. Grill or bake in a moderate oven – four to five minutes each side if grilling, eight to ten minutes if cooked in the oven, depending on the thickness of the fish. Decorate with chopped parsley and serve with more melted butter.

Kippers

Kippers are either dyed brown and then lightly smoked, as are Scottish kippers – dyeing not only cuts down on the time required for smoking but is supposed to help them retain their natural oil and so render them more succulent – or they are undyed and wholly smoked, as are Manx kippers. So far as appearance is concerned the dyed kippers are a most attractive walnut-brown shade while the wholly smoked undyed ones rarely deepen to more than a pale gold colour. I think myself that there is a distinct difference in flavour between dyed and undyed kippers but since I lived for so many years in Scotland and now live in the Isle of Man I refuse to commit myself to stating my own preference, if indeed I have one. I enjoy all kippers so long as they don't come out of a deep freeze or a tin. However, I find that dyed kippers need slightly longer cooking than undyed kippers.

1 pair kippers   Water
Butter

Cut off the heads of the kippers neatly. Put about a quarter to half an inch of water in a shallow baking dish and lay the kippers in it skin side down. Brush the kipper well with soft butter and bake in a hot oven for about six minutes.

Kipper Paste

4 Kippers   2 oz (50 gm) butter

Pick the flesh from the cooked kippers and mince finely. Melt most of the butter in a saucepan, add the minced fish and cook for two minutes. Put into a basin. Melt the remaining butter and pour over the top. This will keep for some days.

To Cook a Manx Kipper (traditional method)

Remove head and tail of kipper and place belly side down in a cold frying pan over a moderate heat. When brown turn and cook for about three minutes. There is no need to grease the frying pan. Serve hot with a small knob of butter on top.

I prefer to spread my kipper with butter and grill for about three minutes on each side.

Mackerel

Mackerel are in my opinion among the tastiest fishes in the sea and given the choice of a plate of fresh mackerel or a plate of fresh salmon I would unhesitatingly choose the mackerel, so that I am surprised when I hear of people who refuse to eat mackerel and deride it as a 'dirty feeder'. On the contrary let me assure you that mackerel are among the cleanest feeding fishes in the sea since they swim mainly neither close to the surface nor on the bottom but in the middle depths of the sea, so common sense must tell us that they do not get a chance to feed on 'dirt' for 'dirt' (a necessary euphemism in a cookery book) either floats or else it sinks. Many of the normally accepted market fish (notably cod and flat fish) do spend their lives on the bottom of the sea, feeding voraciously on anything they can find there. Mackerel do in fact feed mostly on plankton and small fish fry, as anyone who has followed the dark shadows of the mackerel shoals pursuing their rustling agitated prey through the sea will be able to corroborate. I admit that though the seas around Bruach abounded in mackerel during the summer months the Bruachites rarely ate them, but that was because of the Levitical injunction not to eat 'fish without scales'. It is a fallacy that mackerel have no scales, and those of my neighbours who were prepared to disregard the injunction had nothing but praise for the fish.

There are two provisos I would make in regard not only to mackerel but to any other fish I proposed to eat and the first is that they must not have been caught by anglers fishing from sea walls or quays or from boats which stay too close to harbours where there is a likelihood of effluent pouring into the sea. The second is that they must not have been displayed ungutted on a fishmonger's slab. No fish spoils more rapidly than mackerel and the practice of selling ungutted fish I find both abhorrent and inexcusable. However, I fear that many people have become so accustomed to stale fish that, given the opportunity, they would not appreciate the flavour of really fresh fish, as the following true story appears to illustrate.

There came to Bruach one summer a family of campers – father, mother, their two daughters and an aunt – and the father, having watched the local boats go out fishing in an evening, prevailed upon one of the boatmen to let him accompany them. At the end of the evening's fishing when the catch was sorted the man delightedly took home five fish for his family. A couple of nights later he was again taken out fishing but this time when the catch was sorted the man refused to take more than one fish.

'Go on,' insisted the boatman. 'You caught more than that.'

'No, it's no use my taking them. The family refused to eat them. They said they didn't smell like proper fish.'

'There was nothin' wrong with them,' responded the boatman indignantly.

'Oh, no,' the man agreed. 'I got my wife to cook mine and I thoroughly enjoyed it but none of the others would touch it. I'll just take this one for myself.' So he took just his one fish and the following evening again he took one fish out of the evening's catch. A few days later the man went out on another fishing trip and this time he was as keen as anyone to take his full share of the catch.

'So they're after eatin' them now?' probed the boatman, suspecting that the man might be going to sell them to some of the other campers.

'They wouldn't but now I've got an idea. Just let me take these and I promise I'll let you know what happens.'

It was three nights later when the man turned up again to join the boatman and again he was eager to take his share of the catch. The boatman waited for the promised explanation.

'What happened was that the last time I took just the one fish home for myself I put it under a hedge while I called in at the croft along the road for a can of milk. I got talking for a while and I clean forgot about the fish until the next evening. I went and got it but it was getting a bit stinky so I thought I'd take it back to the tent and cook it for the dog. When the wife saw it she said, "Now that's what I call proper fish. I fancy a bit of that." So I didn't tell her I'd brought it thinking to cook it for the dog. When the others smelled it cooking they fancied a bit too and they liked it so much I never got more than a bite or so to give to the dog. They told me if I could bring home fish that was as tasty as that they'd like me to go fishing every evening. So the next time I came out with you I took my share but except for the one fish I kept out for myself I put the lot under the hedge until the next day before I gave it to the family. And they fairly enjoyed every bit of it.'

'I would not be eatin' fish that was after lyin' a day and a night in this weather,' observed the boatman.

'Neither would I,' agreed the man. 'But if they won't eat fish unless it's beginning to get a stink on it then I might just as well provide it for them, seeing it's no trouble.'

You may recognize a fresh mackerel by its sleek, silver–brightness and by the firmness of its flesh when pressed with the finger and should you be fortunate enough to find such fish there are countless recipes for cooking them. The simplest way is to put the whole fish into warm water (boiling water for all fish except mackerel). Bring to the boil and simmer for six to fifteen minutes according to size – they are done when the skin begins to come loose from the flesh.

Mackerel must be lifted carefully out of the water as soon as they are cooked and then left to cool on a dish. They are good served cold with a squeeze of lemon and accompanied by mayonnaise and fresh salad but they are even better served hot with parsley sauce, peas and potatoes. More recipes follow, all of them delectable.

Mackerel Bruach

It is more satisfactory to learn to fillet mackerel yourself rather than ask the fishmonger to do it for you. Here is the method. With a thin sharp-bladed knife make a cut behind the pectoral fin to the backbone, turn the knife, slide it back along the backbone to the tail, leaving the dorsal fin on the backbone. Turn over and repeat on the other side. Wipe with damp kitchen paper, do not wash. Don't worry if the fillets look a bit ragged. Skill will come with practice.

2 whole mackerel (4 fillets)	Salt and pepper
4 oz (100 gm) oatmeal	

Season the oatmeal and press it on to both sides of each fillet. Lightly grease a lidded frying pan and make it moderately hot. Lay each fillet flesh side down in the pan, packing all the fillets in together. Put on the lid. Cook over a low heat, turning when one side is beginning to brown. The cooking time depends on the plumpness of the fillets and the amount of heat but they should be tender and golden when they are ready. Serve 'undressed' or with a home-made tomato sauce.

Mackerel Curry

6 fillets, raw or cooked, of mackerel	1 tablespn flour
2 med. sized onions, chopped	Salt, pepper and cayenne
1 teaspn tomato purée	1 teaspn brown sugar
1 cooking apple, grated	½ pint (300 ml) milk and water,
1 tablespn curry powder	or stock made by boiling
½ teaspn curry paste	mackerel bones in water for
2 oz (50 gm) butter	half an hour

Melt the butter in a saucepan and add the onions. Cook until golden brown. Add the tomato purée, apple, brown sugar, curry powder and paste and cook for a further two minutes. Stir in the flour and add the milk and water or stock slowly. Add the seasoning and cayenne. If using raw mackerel mince the fish and add to the sauce and continue cooking for a further ten minutes. If using cooked mackerel, flake the fish and add it to the sauce and continue cooking for only two minutes.

Mackerel Fillets Bechamel

4 mackerel fillets
¾ pint (450 ml) bechamel sauce

1½ oz (35 gm) butter
1 teaspn lemon juice

Bechamel sauce:

2 oz (50 gm) flour
2 oz (50 gm) butter
1 pint (600 ml) milk
Bouquet garni
Small onion or shallot

Stalk celery
Small bayleaf
Pinch mace
Pinch cayenne pepper

Melt the butter in a saucepan and fry the fillets without browning them for about two minutes. Remove the fillets, sprinkle them with the lemon juice and keep hot.

To make the bechamel sauce, add the vegetables and seasonings to the milk and bring to the boil; set aside for about ten minutes to infuse. Melt the butter, stir in the flour and gradually stir in the strained milk, stirring all the time. Bring to the boil and simmer gently for two to three minutes. Test for seasoning.

Put the mackerel fillets into a casserole, pour over the bechamel sauce and simmer gently or cook in a moderate oven for ten minutes.

Mackerel Pie

1 med. sized onion, chopped
Seasoning
1 oz (25 gm) butter
2 teaspn chopped parsley

4 mackerel fillets
¼ teaspn mustard
Mashed potato, approx. 1 lb (450 gm) when cooked

Put the mackerel fillets into warm water, bring to boil and simmer gently for three minutes. Remove the fish from the water and flake them. Fry the onion in the butter until transparent. Add the fish, parsley, mustard and seasoning. Put into a pie dish. Top with mashed potato sprinkled with parsley and dot with butter. Brown under grill or heat through in a moderate oven.

Mackerel Savoury

6 mackerel fillets
2 oz (50 gm) flour
Seasoning
Med. sized onion (chopped finely)
2 oz (50 gm) butter

Small cupful (150 ml) of stock
   made with chicken-broth cube
2 egg yolks
1 teaspn Worcester sauce or 2
   tablespn port wine
Dessertspn chopped parsley

Boil the onion and parsley together in a little water, drain and add the salt and pepper. Lay the mackerel fillets in a pan or casserole, sprinkle with seasoning. Dot half the butter over the mackerel and add the stock. Put on a tight-fitting lid and simmer or bake in a moderate oven for about twenty minutes. Remove the fish and place on a hot dish. Sprinkle on more seasoning and dot with the remaining butter. Boil up the liquid in the pan or casserole and re-season if necessary. Beat up the two egg yolks. Remove the sauce from the heat and stir in the eggs and the Worcester sauce or port wine. Heat gently until smooth and thick and pour over the fish.

Smoked Mackerel

I can never make up my mind whether smoked mackerel have the edge on kippers for flavour but kippers are easier to find in the shops. However, smoked mackerel are well worth looking out for and if you ask for them repeatedly perhaps they will become more readily available.

1 smoked mackerel per person   Butter
Lemon juice (optional)

Cut off the head of the mackerel. Put the fish into a shallow pan and just cover with warm water. Bring to the boil, simmer gently for two minutes. Drain off the water, brush with melted butter and either grill for three minutes each side or cover with foil and bake in a hot oven for ten to fifteen minutes according to size. Sprinkle with lemon juice before serving.

Mock Whitebait (made with haddock, plaice or whiting)

2 whiting, filleted (four fillets)	Salt and pepper
2 tablespn flour	Chopped parsley

Remove the skin from the fish and cut up the fillets into small pieces about two inches long and half an inch wide. Season the flour with the salt and pepper and roll the pieces of fish in it. Shake off the surplus flour and drop one by one into hot fat. Fry until crisp and golden brown. Sprinkle with chopped parsley.

Monk Fish

This fish is likely to appear more frequently on the fishmongers' slabs as the familiar varieties become scarcer. Why 'monk fish' I do not know, since prolonged inspection convinces me there is nothing about its appearance that resembles a monk. It is, however, one of the species known as 'angler fish', so called because they have a modified front dorsal spine which hangs over the mouth like a baited fishing rod on which they catch their prey. As monks are associated with angling I can only surmise that this is why it has come to be known as 'monk'. Its mouth is almost as wide as its body but only the thick 'tail' of the fish is marketed. It is good value for money and I believe in restaurants it is often cut up into strips about three inches by one inch, dipped in batter and served as scampi. I doubt if I would be fooled but nevertheless I can vouch for the fact that it is quite delicious when prepared in this way. It is also nice in casseroles. Here are two more ways of cooking it.

Baked Monk Fish

2 slices of monk fish tail	1 tablespn chopped parsley
2 oz (50 gm) butter	½ pint (300 ml) of milk
2 large onions	4 slices streaky bacon
Pepper and salt	2 oz (50 gm) flour

Wipe the fish and dry with kitchen paper. Mix the seasonings with the flour and coat the fish. Place them in a greased baking dish. Slice the onions and separate the rings. Dip them in the seasoned flour and fry in the hot butter until golden brown. Lift them out and keep hot. Stir the remainder of the flour into the butter and add the milk, stirring all the time. Boil for one minute, add the parsley and pour over the fish. Put into the oven and bake for fifteen minutes. Take out of the oven, lay the onion slices on top and cover with strips of bacon. Return to the oven and continue baking for another fifteen minutes or until the fish is cooked through.

Monk Fish Casserole

1 lb (450 gm) monk fish	2 tomatoes
1 tablespn flour	1 cup (100 ml) water
Salt and pepper	Pinch mixed herbs
2 oz (50 gm) dripping	1 teaspn Worcester sauce
2 onions	¼ teaspn gravy browning
¼ lb (100 gm) mushrooms	

Wipe the fish and cut into three or four portions. Toss in the seasoned flour and fry until light brown on both sides. Put the fish in a casserole. Fry the sliced onions in the dripping until they are well browned and add them to the fish. Fry the sliced mushrooms and sliced tomatoes and put in the casserole. Sprinkle the rest of the seasoned flour into the melted dripping in the saucepan, stir and cook for one minute; add the water, herbs, and Worcester sauce. Taste and add more salt and pepper if necessary. Bring to the boil, stirring. Colour with the gravy browning and pour over the fish in the casserole. Put on the lid and bake in a moderately hot oven for about half an hour. Serve with mashed potatoes.

Saithe

Saithe, or lythe, or coalie as it is sometimes called, is described as being a fish 'of no commercial value', i.e. neither fish salesmen nor fishmongers will buy it so when their nets come up full of saithe more often than not the fishermen throw their catch back into the sea. This seems a pity because apart from its colour – it tends to be slightly grey-fleshed in comparison with cod – saithe is in fact quite a palatable fish. Cooked in accordance with the following instructions it is really appetizing.

4 saithe fillets	Flour to coat fish
2 oz (50 gm) butter	Salt and pepper
1 glass white wine	¼ lb (100 gm) fresh breadcrumbs
Good pinch sweet basil	1 oz (25 gm) flaked almonds

Mix the flour, salt and pepper together and coat the fillets. Melt half of the butter in a casserole and fry the fish lightly for about one minute each side. Add wine and basil. Put the lid on the casserole and cook in a moderately hot oven for about twenty to thirty minutes according to the thickness of the fillets. Meanwhile mix together the breadcrumbs and flaked nuts, season with salt and pepper. Melt the remaining butter in a frying pan. Put in the crumb and nut mixture and fry until just beginning to turn brown. Serve with the fish.

Salmon

I have only once in my life eaten a legally caught salmon and this is the way I cooked and served it. But I still think illicit salmon has a more piquant flavour.

Scrape the scales from the fish and wash away any blood. Sprinkle it lightly with salt and put into a steamer allowing twenty minutes to the pound and twenty minutes over. When the fish is cooked the flesh should come away easily from the bone. Drain and serve with Hollandaise sauce.

Hollandaise Sauce

¼ lb (100 gm) butter cut into small pieces	2 egg yolks
	Salt, pepper, and lemon juice

Put half the butter in a basin over hot water and when the butter is melted add the egg yolks, well beaten. Stir until the sauce begins to thicken and then add the rest of the butter piece by piece. The sauce should now be of a creamy consistency. Add the seasonings and lemon juice. Keep hot but ensure sauce does not boil.

I thought bought salmon was worth the effort of making a true Hollandaise sauce for, but normally I use a mock Hollandaise which is made by whisking a whole egg into an ordinary white sauce and then adding a teaspoon of lemon juice.

Salmon may also be boiled. Put the whole fish into near-boiling salted water – about one level teaspoon salt per pint of water. Simmer gently, allowing ten minutes to the pound and ten minutes over.

Slices or cutlets of salmon are best grilled. Ideally they should be about one inch thick. Wipe the cutlets, dry them and dip in melted butter or salad oil. Have the grill pan thoroughly hot, grease it, put in the fish and cook under the grill. After five minutes turn the fish and again after five minutes turn, allowing ten minutes for each side. Serve with a slice of lemon, a sprinkling of parsley and either true or mock Hollandaise sauce.

Salmon Soufflé

3 oz (75 gm) flour	1 teaspn lemon juice
Half pint (300 ml) milk	Pinch nutmeg
1 oz (25 gm) butter	1 oz (25 gm) browned bread-
4 oz (100 gm) tin salmon	crumbs
2 eggs	Salt

Flake the salmon with a fork. Blend flour and milk to a smooth cream in a saucepan. Add the butter and salt and cook until the mixture begins to leave the sides of the pan. Remove from the heat. Stir the lightly beaten eggs, the lemon juice and nutmeg into the flaked salmon and mix thoroughly with the sauce. Put into a greased soufflé dish and sprinkle the top with breadcrumbs. Bake in a moderate oven until nicely browned (about twenty minutes).

Salmon Tart

6 oz (175 gm) shortcrust pastry   Parsley sauce
4 oz (100 gm) tin salmon   Pinch nutmeg
Salt and pepper

Line a pie dish with the pastry, saving any trimmings for decoration, and bake blind in a hot oven until golden brown. Flake the salmon with a fork. Season with salt and pepper and a tiny pinch of nutmeg. Make the parsley sauce, using the liquor from the salmon in addition to milk. Gradually stir in enough sauce to the flaked salmon to make it easily spread and put into the pastry case. Smooth the top and decorate with strips of pastry arranged lattice fashion and brushed with milk. Bake in a moderate oven for ten minutes. Serve with the remaining parsley sauce.

Salt Herring

Until a few years ago no Bruach crofter would have dreamed of facing the winter without a good barrel of salt herring in his store. For the islander salt herring and potatoes is not just a basic food but almost a revered one: a treat that ex-patriots dream of returning home to: a feast that any prodigal son would prefer to a fatted calf.

I too, while in Bruach, regularly stored my quarter barrel of salt herring and though initially I regarded them as an emergency food to be endured when nothing more palatable was available time and necessity helped me to develop a moderate liking for them, though I prefer them de-salted before cooking by being soaked for a few hours in at least three changes of fresh water.

In the Isle of Man, too, salt herring and tatties is a traditional dish and even today a herring and tattie supper is a popular event. The only difference seems to be that while in the Isle of Man the recommended accompaniment to tatties and herring is raw onion and a glass of buttermilk in Scotland it is inevitably a glass of whisky.

Salt herrings are supposed to be extremely good for one

and Norwegian fishermen are so fond of drinking the 'bree', the mixture of salt oil and juices left in the bottom of the herring barrels, that they are reputed to try to bribe employees at the curing yards to save the liquor for them rather than just throw it down the drain as normally happens in this country. They believe it has therapeutic qualities, curing everything from a cold to a hangover. 'It does a lot for a man,' one of them told me, but from my observation all I have seen it do for them is to give them a magnificent thirst.

Salt Herring and 'Tatties'

Salt herring	Potatoes (unpeeled)

Remove the heads from the herring.
Wash the herring and leave in cold water for one hour (I prefer mine to soak overnight with at least three changes of water during that time). Scrub the potatoes and put them into a large saucepan. Cover with plenty of water (unsalted) and bring to the boil. When boiling put in the herring. Remove the fish when cooked (about fifteen to twenty minutes according to size) and keep hot until the potatoes have finished cooking. Serve with plenty of fresh butter.

Turbot

1 med. sized turbot (filleted and skinned)	1 glass dry white wine
1 oz (25 gm) butter	¼ lb (100 gm) small mushrooms
1 tablespn flour	1 teaspn chopped parsley
½ teaspn salt	Lemon slices for garnish
¼ teaspn pepper	1 teaspn grated horseradish
Pinch sweet basil	(optional)

Mix together the salt, pepper and sweet basil. Use half the butter to grease the casserole and sprinkle over half the seasoning. Put in the turbot and sprinkle with the remainder of the seasoning. Dredge with flour. Add the white wine and the mushrooms. Dot with the remaining butter and bake in a moderate oven for twenty to thirty minutes according to the size of the turbot. When cooked sprinkle with chopped parsley and decorate with lemon slices. Serve with a sprinkle of grated horseradish if liked and with shrimp sauce. Fingers of crisp fried bread are also a nice accompaniment to turbot.

Turbot-roe Paste

If you are fortunate enough to find roe in your turbot use it to make a sandwich filling thus:

1 lb (450 gm) roe (blanched in boiling water for two minutes)	Pinch mace
	Pinch tarragon
1 tablespn lemon juice	Salt, pepper and garlic salt
3 oz (75 gm) butter	¼ teaspn chopped parsley

Melt the butter in the saucepan and add the pounded or mashed roe. Stir in the lemon juice and season to taste. Cook over gentle heat for two minutes.

Whiting

Whiting is considered to be a somewhat tasteless fish though it is very light and easily digested. Try it this way:

4 fillets (2 whole fish)	Salt and pepper
Oatmeal (not rolled oats)	

Wipe the fish with kitchen paper – damp paper if you like but don't ever wash fish except in sea water. If the fish doesn't look clean enough to eat without being washed then don't buy it!

Dip each fillet in the seasoned oatmeal and put into shallow hot fat belly side down (the white underside); fry quickly until golden brown then turn and similarly brown the other side.

Alternatively the oatmeal dipped fillets can be placed in a buttered dish with a lid and baked in a hot oven for about fifteen minutes. Serve with home-made tomato sauce (page 191).

Crisped Whiting

4 whiting fillets	1 teaspn oil
1 egg white	Salt and pepper
2 tablespn flour	Fat for frying

Brush the whiting over with the oil and season with pepper and salt. Lightly beat the egg white and dip the fillets. Dredge with flour and fry in hot fat until crisp and lightly browned.

Marinaded Whiting

6 fillets whiting	1 tablespn dry white wine
2 tablespns oil	1 teaspn chopped parsley
Salt and pepper	Fat for frying

Batter:

2 oz (50 gm) flour	2 tablespns oil
¼ pint (150 ml) milk (or milk and water)	Pinch salt
	Whites of 2 eggs

Mix the oil, pepper, salt, wine and parsley together and pour over the fillets. Let them lie in the marinade for about two hours. Drain them and dip them in the batter. Fry in hot fat until golden brown (be sure not to overcook whiting). Drain on crumpled kitchen paper on a hot dish.

Batter: Sieve the flour and salt into a bowl and make a well in the centre. Mix the milk, or milk and water and oil together and stir gradually into the mixture. Leave in a cool place for an hour if possible. Meanwhile beat the egg whites until stiff and fold into the batter just before using.

Smoked whiting make lovely kedgerees:

Kedgeree

4 oz (100 gm) butter	¼ teaspn black pepper
10 oz (275 gm) cooked smoked fish, skinned, boned and flaked	¼ teaspn cayenne pepper
4 oz (100 gm) rice	¼ pint (150 ml) single cream
2 hard-boiled eggs	Chopped parsley
Half teaspn salt	1 oz (25 gm) grated cheese

Boil rice, and drain. Chop the eggs finely. Melt three ounces (75 gm) of the butter in a saucepan. Add the cooked rice, the fish, seasonings and hard-boiled eggs. Stir in the cream. Put in serving dish, dot with remaining butter and sprinkle with cheese. Brown under grill, sprinkle with chopped parsley and serve.

Meat, Poultry and Game

Looking back through my old Bruach notebooks I came across an entry headed 'Donald Bhan's Bad Cow, Recipes for'. It was dated 24th March 1950 and immediately I recalled that unspringlike day of chilly drizzle when Donald's cow (dubbed 'bad' because of its persistent fence-breaking), strayed too near the edge of the cliff and plunged to its death on the shore below. The loss of a cow is a sad blow to the crofter who may own only one or two cows, and since this was a young beast, neither in milk nor in calf and the flesh was therefore likely to be in near prime condition, the resourceful Donald announced he was going to try to recoup part of his loss by butchering the carcass and selling the meat for sixpence a pound. The tide was beginning to flow when the beast fell and so whatever butchering could be done had to be done quickly before the sea claimed the animal and since it would have been not only wasteful but also unneighbourly to turn their backs on the bargain Donald offered, the crofters scurried for pails and bowls. While Donald chopped and hacked they piled their receptacles high with great lumps of meat that were still flabby in their freshness.

I was too ashamed to ask for the small quantity I estimated I could use, so I proffered five shillings and took only one pail to hold my purchase. But the amount of meat on a cow is truly prodigious and as Donald was far too proud to take my five shillings and give me less than five shillings' worth of meat in return I felt I dared not demur when, after filling my pail for the first time, he insisted I came back for more. What I had not reckoned on was that though he was charging sixpence a pound for the prime cuts the lesser ones were going for a penny a pound and as a consequence I ended up with well over thirty pounds of meat plus the heart, liver and kidneys, along with great wads of suet no one else wanted. It took me three journeys to carry home my haul and when I surveyed my kitchen table covered with the gory burden which now had to be disposed of I reflected that Donald Bhan's bad cow looked like proving as much a nuisance in death as she had been in life.

I ate beef, baked and boiled, casseroled and curried for as long as I could enjoy it. The hens ate so much liver and kidney that not just the shells of their eggs were brown, the yolks too took on a distinct ochre colour. I looked for ways to preserve the rest of the meat and since electricity and refrigeration were still a long way from Bruach and since I was not prepared to do as the crofters did, i.e. put the meat in a barrel between generous layers of coarse salt, I ferreted out an old cookery book. With its help I successfully pickled several joints, of which 'Hunter's Beef' turned out to be the tastiest. The recipe I used takes its place in this chapter just in case the day should come when you too are offered 'casualty cow' perhaps in larger quantities than you can immediately use.

Beef Casserole with Dumplings

1 lb (450 gm) stewing beef	2 oz (50 gm) flour
1 large onion	Salt and pepper
¼ turnip	1 dessertspn Worcester sauce
3 carrots	Bouquet garni
1 stalk celery	Gravy browning

Cut the meat into pieces. Slice the vegetables and shred the celery. Add the seasoning to the flour and toss the meat and vegetables in it. Put the meat and vegetables into a casserole. Add the sauce and bouquet garni and barely cover with cold water. Put on the lid and bake in a moderate oven for about two hours until meat is almost tender. Remove the casserole from the oven and take out the bouquet garni. Add the gravy browning. Taste for seasoning and add the dumplings.

Dumplings:

4 oz (100 gm) flour
1 teaspn baking powder
½ teaspn salt
Pinch pepper

2 oz (50 gm) shredded suet
Small pinch mixed herbs
Cold water to mix

Mix the dry ingredients together with the suet. Add cold water and mix quickly to a firm, light dough. Shape into balls and put into casserole. Replace lid and cook for about twenty minutes.

Beef Stroganoff

¾ lb (350 gm) steak (preferably fillet)
¼ lb (100 gm) small mushrooms
1 med. size onion
1 oz (25 gm) butter
1 tablespn oil

¼ pint (150 ml) or more thick fresh cream (with two teaspns lemon juice to sour) or ¼ pint (150 ml) sour cream
Salt and pepper

Slice steak into thin strips. Chop onion very small and slice the mushrooms. Heat butter and oil in a large heavy-based frying pan. Put in onion and mushrooms, cook until onion is transparent. Cook on high heat, add meat and continue cooking and stirring for two minutes or a little longer according to taste. Remove from heat. Pour in the sour cream or the cream and lemon juice if used, about half a teaspoon salt and a liberal dusting of black pepper, freshly ground if possible. Bubble up over a good heat, stir and serve straight away. Chopped parsley sprinkled over the dish makes it taste and look even better.

Bullock or Ox Heart, Stuffed and Roasted

1 bullock (or ox) heart
4 oz (100 gm) sage & onion stuffing
1 egg

1 rasher bacon
2 oz (50 gm) soft dripping
Salt and pepper

Soak the heart for about two hours in cold, salted water, then wash out the coagulated blood under cold running water.

Chop the bacon into small pieces. Moisten the stuffing with egg and water and stir the bacon into this. Add seasoning. Use the mixture for stuffing the heart. Rub the dripping over the heart, wrap in foil and roast in a moderate oven for three to four hours according to the size of the heart.

Serve with rich brown gravy and apple sauce.

The same stuffing and method can be used for sheep's hearts.

Curry and Rice

I firmly believe that the flavour of a curry is enhanced by being cooked, left to cool for a few hours, or even overnight and then re-heated. This makes it an ideal dish to prepare in advance.

1 lb (450 gm) minced beef	1 oz (25 gm) sultanas
2 oz (50 gm) dripping	1 teaspn lime juice
2 med. sized onions	1 banana
1 med. size apple	1 tablespn Indian chutney
1 teaspn curry paste	1 tablespn plain flour
1 teaspn curry powder (more if liked)	¾ pint (450 ml) stock
	1 teaspn brown sugar
1 dessertspn tomato sauce or chutney	1 teaspn turmeric
	Salt and pepper
1 oz (25 gm) salted peanuts	

Peel and chop or mince coarsely the onions, apple and nuts.

Heat the dripping and fry the onions and apple until pale brown. Remove from the fat and add the minced beef. Fry for about five minutes, stirring it all the time. Remove from the fat. Put in the tomato sauce, curry paste, and curry powder and cook for about one minute. Add the nuts, Indian chutney, sultanas, brown sugar, banana and lime juice. Cook for one minute, then add the flour and stock gradually. Bring to the boil, add the meat, apple, onions and turmeric. Season with salt and pepper. Cover and simmer for one hour.

Serve with rice, sliced hard-boiled eggs and onion badjis (page 205).

If using ready-cooked beef stir this in about ten minutes before the rest of the curry has finished cooking.

Goulash

1 lb (450 gm) stewing steak	3 med. sized carrots, diced
1 large onion, sliced	1 stalk celery, chopped or minced
1 oz (25 gm) dripping	Piece turnip, about ¼ lb (100 gm)
1 oz (25 gm) plain flour	diced
Pepper and salt	6 mushrooms
1 dessertspn tomato purée	1 teaspn Worcester sauce
1 teaspn turmeric	Bouquet garni
1 pint (600 ml) stock or water	

Heat the dripping until smoking hot. Stir in the sliced onion and fry until golden brown. Cut the meat into bite-sized pieces, roll in the seasoned flour and put into the hot fat with the onion. Keep stirring and allow the meat to sizzle for about two minutes. Take out the meat and onion. Stir the tomato purée and the turmeric into the pan; add the remainder of the seasoned flour in which the meat was rolled; cook and stir until light brown. Add the stock and bring to the boil. Return meat and onions to the pan, add the vegetables, the sauce and the bouquet garni. Taste for seasoning. Cover and simmer slowly for two hours either on top of the cooker or in a moderate oven. Remove bouquet garni before serving.

Hotpot

1 lb (450 gm) stewing steak	3 large onions
2 oz (50 gm) flour	1½ lb (675 gm) potatoes
Salt and pepper	¾ pint (450 ml) stock or water
1 level teaspn turmeric	½ oz (15 gm) dripping

Mix the salt, pepper and turmeric with the flour. Cut the meat into neat pieces and roll in the seasoned flour. Peel and slice the onions and potatoes about half an inch thick. Put half the onion slices into a casserole, top with half the meat and then half the potatoes. Add another layer of onion, meat and potatoes. Pour in the stock and dot the top potato layer with small pieces of dripping. Put the lid on the casserole and bake in a moderate oven for two hours. Remove the lid and continue baking for another twenty minutes until the potatoes are nicely browned.

Hunter's Beef

Piece of beef weighing about seven pounds.

For the pickle:	Pinch nutmeg
1 oz (25 gm) saltpetre	Pinch allspice
1 oz (35 gm) brown sugar	6 oz (175 gm) coarse salt
4 cloves	
For cooking the beef after pickling:	1 lb (450 gm) plain flour
¼ lb (100 gm) shredded suet	½ pint (300 ml) water

Crush the cloves and mix with the rest of the pickle ingredients. Rub into the beef every day for three weeks. At the end of that time bandage it tightly with strips of cheesecloth so it will keep its shape. Keep in a cool place.

When you want to cook it remove the bandaging and put the beef into a deep dish with half a pint (300 ml) of cold water. Sprinkle the top with suet. Make a paste with flour and water and cover the dish. Bake in a moderate oven for about three hours, testing after two hours to see if it is tender. (The skewer should go through without resistance.) Do not remove the paste until the dish has been cooling for about half an hour.

Lumberjack Beef

3 lb (1 kg) round of beef (approx.)	¾ pint (450 ml) stock
1 teaspn oil	Salt and pepper, pinch of cayenne
1 oz (25 gm) butter	Wineglass Madeira or similar wine
1 oz (25 gm) flour	12 button mushrooms

Brush the beef with oil and put into a hot oven. Cook for half an hour. Meanwhile prepare a sauce by melting the butter in a saucepan large enough to take the beef, stirring in the flour, seasonings and stock. Bring to the boil, add the wine and keep hot. Put the half-cooked beef into the saucepan, add the mushrooms and cook slowly for another hour or until the beef is tender.

In my youth every winter brought a crop of posters on church notice boards and in shop windows announcing 'A Potato Pie Supper and Entertainment'. Such suppers were favourite church fund-raising events (as also were 'hot-pot' suppers) and since I loved potato pie whenever I had a spare shilling and nothing more important to do I would be off, escorted by Janet, our maid, to the Congregational Church Hall or the Methodist or Salvation Army or Roman Catholic Church Halls to sample their food and entertainment. The entertainment was unvaried; the potato pies ranged from the mediocre to the appetizing, though none of them could ever compete in my opinion with the pies my mother used to make. Thick-crusted and mushy inside, I think my mother's pies were probably stodgy and indigestible, but that was the way I liked them and she must have been flattered when, time after time, I would come home from a potato pie supper and in reply to her casually asked question would say, 'It wasn't bad. But nowhere near as good as home-made,' or 'It was awful, nothing but potato in it.' I did not realize then how much pleasure my condemnation of other people's pies must have given her, although I was sensible of the fact that always, within two or three days of my making such comments, my father, who liked to eat his meat in slices off the joint, would have to endure having meat-and-potato pie for dinner simply because his daughter liked it so much. Since those days my tastes have changed more than a little and I now prefer my meat and potato pies to be lighter and 'gravier'. Like rabbit pie, I make it in two stages, cooking the meat the day before.

Meat-and-potato Pie

Pastry:
½ lb (225 gm) S.R. flour
Pinch salt

¼ lb (100 gm) lard
Water to mix

Filling:

1 lb (450 gm) potatoes when peeled	1 oz (25 gm) dripping
1 lb (450 gm) shin of beef	1 large onion, chopped
1 tablespn plain flour	1 pint (600 ml) stock
Salt and pepper	1 med. size carrot
	½ teaspn Worcester sauce

Cut the meat into bite-size pieces. Sieve the plain flour and salt and pepper together and toss the meat in this. Melt the dripping and fry the meat until just beginning to brown. Take out the meat and fry the onion until brown. Put the meat and onion into a pan, cover with stock and bring to the boil. When boiling add the sliced carrot and sliced potatoes and the Worcester sauce. Re-boil and simmer for two hours, adding more stock if necessary. Leave to cool.

Sieve the S.R. flour and the salt together. Rub in the lard finely and mix with water to a nice elastic dough. Roll out to half-and-inch thickness.

Put the cooked meat with about half the gravy into a pie dish – the gravy should not come more than halfway up. With a draining spoon lift out most of the carrot and potato and lay them on the meat. Top with the pastry. Make a ventilation hole in the top or better still use an old-fashioned 'pie-thief' (a pot funnel) and bake in a moderate oven for thirty minutes or until the pastry is nicely brown. Heat the remaining gravy and top up pie before serving.

Mixed Grill

Per person allow:

1 piece of fillet steak (about ¼ lb) (100 gm)	1 rasher of bacon
	1 tomato
½ kidney	3 mushrooms
1 sausage	Oil or melted butter
	Salt and pepper

Split the kidneys lengthwise down to the 'root', remove the skin. Brush the steak and kidney with butter or oil, season and grill together with the sausage. (Always grill the cut side of the kidney first.) Turn after three minutes and cook other side. When cooked keep hot while you grill the mushrooms, previously brushed with melted butter or oil, the bacon and the tomatoes. Serve with chipped potatoes.

Baked Steak with Bananas

1 lb (450 gm) braising steak cut in one piece about 1 in. thick (2 cm)	Pepper, salt
	Teaspn brown sugar
	Shake of nutmeg
3 bananas	

Cut through the steak so that it opens out like a book (leaving one side uncut, like a hinge). Season with salt, pepper and nutmeg. Peel and cut the bananas lengthwise and lay them on one side of the steak. Sprinkle the sugar over the bananas. Fold over the steak (close the book) and 'sew' a skewer through the two edges, fastening them together. Put into a casserole with about an eighth of a pint of water or stock and bake in a moderately hot oven for about one hour.

Grilled Steak with Banana Stuffing

2 pieces of fillet steak about 1 to 1½ in. (3 cm)	¼ lb (100 gm) button mushrooms
Salt and pepper	2 tomatoes, skinned and sliced
1 garlic clove, crushed	Oil or dripping
1 banana	Melted butter

Season the steak on both sides with salt and pepper and rub over with crushed garlic. Brush with oil or melted dripping. Grease the grill; lay the meat on it and grill for about two minutes until browned (the grill should be fairly hot). Turn the steak with a spatula (never stick a fork into steak which is being cooked) and grill for two minutes on the other side. Reduce the heat of the grill and continue cooking, turning several times, allowing a total of twelve minutes for rare, fifteen minutes for medium rare, but up to thirty minutes if you want it to be well done.

Meanwhile peel and slice the banana lengthwise; fry the mushrooms and tomatoes. Brush the banana with melted butter and brown under the grill. Place the banana slices on top of the steak and garnish with mushrooms and tomatoes.

Peppered Steak with Brandy

4 pieces rump steak	1 tablespn oil
Black pepper	2 tablespns brandy
3 oz (75 gm) butter	¼ pint (150 ml) double cream

Dredge the steaks both sides with the pepper. Heat the butter and oil in a frying pan and cook for five to ten minutes, according to your taste, and turning them halfway. Lift out of the frying pan and keep warm on a dish. Add the brandy to the hot fat and juices in the frying pan and set alight. Remove from the heat immediately and stir in the cream. Heat again gently, season if necessary and pour over the steaks.

Steak-and-Kidney Pudding

1 lb (450 gm) stewing steak	¼ teaspn pepper
2 sheep's kidneys	1 onion
1 pigeon (optional)	1 teaspn chopped parsley
1 heaped tablespn flour	Stock or water
¼ teaspn salt	

Pastry:

	4 oz (100 gm) shredded suet
8 oz (225 gm) plain flour	Pinch salt
1 rounded teaspn baking powder	Water to mix

Cut the meat into bite-size pieces and beat them with a steak hammer to make them more tender. Cut the core from the kidneys and remove skin. Cut into small pieces. Joint the pigeon. Toss steak, kidney and pigeon joints in seasoned flour.

Make the pastry by sieving together the flour, salt and baking powder. Add the suet and mix. Add water while quickly mixing to a soft dough. Line an eight-inch greased pudding basin with three-quarters of the dough, reserving the remainder for the 'lid'. Fill the basin with the meat; add the finely chopped onion and about half a cupful of cold

76

stock or water. Roll out the remaining pastry, moisten the edges of the basin and place the paste over the top. (The paste should be larger than the top of the basin.) Cover with greaseproof paper, then with a cloth. Tie tightly. Put into a pan of boiling water, ensuring that the water does not come up more than two-thirds of the sides of the basin. Boil for three hours. Make a hole in the lid just before serving and pour in a little boiling stock. Garnish with parsley.

Stuffed Vegetable Marrow

1 med. sized marrow	Salt and pepper
½ lb (225 gm) minced beef	Pinch mixed herbs
1½ oz (35 gm) dripping or butter	1 egg
2 oz (50 gm) breadcrumbs	Approx. ½ cup (50 ml) stock or
1 med. size onion (minced)	water

Garnish:	¼ lb (100 gm) mushrooms (fried)
4 tomatoes (baked)	1 teaspn parsley, chopped

Melt half an ounce (10 gm) of the dripping or butter in a saucepan and fry the minced beef lightly. Add the breadcrumbs, onions, seasoning and herbs. Mix together over a low heat. Cool slightly and stir in the beaten egg. Add just enough cold water or stock to moisten thoroughly.

Lay the marrow in a baking dish and cut a wedge from the top so that you can scrape all the seeds from the centre of the marrow. Fill the hollow with the meat and breadcrumb mixture and replace the wedge.

Rub the remaining fat over the marrow (there is no need to skin the marrow) and cover with greaseproof paper or foil and bake in a moderate oven for about one hour. Remove paper or foil and continue cooking for a further twenty to thirty minutes until the inside of the marrow is quite tender. Place on a hot dish and garnish with baked tomatoes and mushrooms. Sprinkle with parsley and serve with a rich, brown gravy.

In my opinion the best-flavoured mutton comes from sheep which have been feeding on heathery moorland and which are aged between two and four years. Lamb I find flavourless in comparison. Every autumn in Bruach those crofters who owned sheep would kill one or two for their own consumption and since it was traditional to share with one's neighbours I was frequently the recipient of a nice joint. Although I had a modern, solid-fuel cooker in my kitchen I had an open fire in my living room and while on holiday in England I had been lucky enough to find in an antique shop an old roasting jack in perfect working order. It became mine for ten shillings and subsequently whenever I was given or could purchase a sizeable joint of mutton I liked to stoke up a big fire of driftwood and peat, hang my joint on the jack and watch and baste as it turned and spat and cooked in the good old-fashioned way while I constantly replenished the fire with more and more wood and peat in compliance with the instruction in the old cookery book to 'roast before a brisk, sharp fire'. It was warm work, but since it was only in cold weather that the meat was available it was by no means a disagreeable task.

The first time I used the roasting jack I feared the experiment was going to prove a dismal failure because the joint stayed raw-looking for so long. However, shortly before the recommended cooking time was up it began to brown quickly on the outside, leading me to the conclusion that spit-roasted meat cooked in front of an open fire must cook from the inside-out – a kind of infra-red process. When finally the meat was ready the flavour was such that I vowed I would always keep an open fire and my roasting jack would be maintained in good working order. It is a vow I have kept despite the fact that I now live in a centrally heated house.

If you have a roasting jack or spit you would like to use and you haven't a recipe book ancient enough to tell you how to set about it here is the method I use.

A leg of mutton is the best joint to cook this way because the sinew makes such a handy loop to hook on the roasting jack. Allow fifteen minutes to the pound and fifteen minutes over. Rub the leg with salt and pepper and put it in front of a 'brisk, sharp fire' (I can think of no better description). Draw it close to the fire for the first ten minutes and then bring it back so that it roasts more slowly. On the hearth under the joint place a large baking tin, dusted lightly with seasoned flour to catch the gravy and fat. My recipe book says 'baste continuously' but not being able to hire a 'basting boy' to do this for me I compromised by basting frequently. Twenty minutes before estimated cooking time is up dredge the meat with flour, baste again and move it nearer the fire so that the skin browns evenly. Pour off the fat from the gravy and add a little hot water to the tin. Season to taste.

If possible contrive some sort of screen behind the joint to reflect the heat when cooking.

Roast Leg of Mutton

Since I do not like vinegar I sometimes marinade the mutton for a few hours before cooking with a mixture of chopped mint, oil, lemon juice, salt and pepper. It would be a crime to marinade Hebridean mutton this way.

1 leg mutton	2 or 3 mint or bayleaves (if liked)
Salt and pepper	Oil

Rub the leg with salt and pepper. Brush with oil and press the mint or bayleaves, if used, into the flesh. Wrap in foil, put into baking tin and cook in a hot oven, allowing twenty minutes to the pound and twenty minutes over. Remove foil and return to oven for a further twenty to thirty minutes until nicely crisp and brown. Serve with onion sauce and savoury mutton pies (page 206).

Boiled Leg of Mutton with Caper Sauce

Small leg mutton	4 carrots
Boiling water	1 turnip, about ¾ lb (350 gm)
Salt and pepper	4 med. sized onions

Put the meat into enough boiling water to completely cover. Bring again to the boil and continue to boil for five minutes. Add salt and pepper to taste. Slice the vegetables thickly and add. Reduce the heat and allow pan to simmer until the meat is cooked (twenty minutes to the pound and twenty minutes over). Ten minutes before cooking time is complete prepare the caper sauce (page 188).

Boston Baked Beans

6 oz (175 gm) haricot beans	1 tablespn brown sugar
1 pound pork pieces	1 dessertspn tomato purée
2 stalks celery shredded or minced	1 tablespn treacle
1 large carrot, sliced thinly	½ teaspn dry mustard
	Pepper and salt

Soak the haricot beans overnight in cold water and drain them. Place the pork pieces in a casserole and cover with the beans. Add the vegetables and sprinkle in the brown sugar. Mix the tomato purée with a cup of warm water and stir in the treacle, mustard, pepper and salt. Pour over the dish and add more water if necessary so as to barely cover the beans. Cover with a lid and bake in a slow oven for about four hours, adding more water from time to time as necessary. About one hour before the dish is cooked remove the lid and bring the pieces of pork above the surface of the beans. Return to the oven and continue cooking for a further hour when the pork should be crisped on the outside. Serve at once.

Pork Casserole

1½ lb (¾ kg) loin of pork	¾ pint (250 ml) stock
1 oz. (25 gm) dripping	Salt and pepper
2 small onions	¼ teaspn mixed mustard
¾ lb (250 gm) cooking apples	Pinch dried sage
1 oz (25 gm) flour	

Divide the meat into chops. Melt the dripping in a frying pan: peel and slice the onions and apples into rings and fry until golden brown. Remove the onion and apple rings and fry the chops for one minute on either side. Remove the chops from the pan and keep hot. Stir in the flour, adding more dripping to mix if necessary and cook until the flour is nicely browned. Stir in the stock and bring to the boil. Add the salt, pepper and mustard. Place the chops in a casserole, cover with the fried apple and onion rings, sprinkle with the sage and pour in the contents of the pan. Cover with a lid and cook in a slow oven for about one and a half hours.

Pork Chops with Sauce Robert

4 pork chops $\frac{1}{2}$ in. (1 cm) thick	Salt and pepper
1 teaspn cooking oil	

Brush the chops lightly with the oil, season with salt and pepper and grill quickly first one side and then the other. Lower the heat of the grill and continue cooking and turning until the chops are well cooked – fifteen to twenty minutes. Keep hot while you make the sauce.

Sauce Robert

1 oz (25 gm) butter	$\frac{1}{2}$ pint (300 ml) stock
2 med. sized onions	1 meat cube
$\frac{1}{2}$ oz (15 gm) flour	$\frac{1}{4}$ teaspn mixed mustard
Salt and pepper	

Melt the butter in a saucepan. Slice the onion and fry in the butter until golden brown. Add the flour and stir while cooking for about two minutes. Add salt and pepper, the stock and the meat cube and stir in the mustard. Bring the sauce to the boil and simmer for about fifteen minutes. Lay the chops in a shallow serving dish and pour the hot sauce over them.

Apple sauce should be served in addition to the Sauce Robert.

Pork Special

About 3 lb (1 kg) loin of pork	½ teaspn black pepper
1 shallot, minced	3 tablespns salad oil
Salt	1 dessertspn chopped parsley

Mix the shallot, black pepper, salt, parsley and oil together and rub them well into the pork. Put the pork into a casserole and bake in a moderately hot oven for about two hours until the pork is well cooked. Baste two or three times during cooking. Place on a hot dish. Serve with the following sauce.

Pork Special Sauce

1 med. sized apple	¼ teaspn cayenne pepper
1 small onion	½ teaspn dry mustard
Fat (from casserole)	1 teaspn sugar
1 teacupful stock	Juice of one lemon
Pinch salt	1 tablespn brandy

Chop the apple and onion finely and fry them in the fat until they are tender but not browned. Mash them well together. Add the stock, all the seasonings, sugar and lemon juice. Bring to the boil and simmer for two minutes. Just before serving add the brandy. Pour half the sauce over the loin and serve the rest separately. Apple sauce should also be served with this dish.

Roast Loin of Pork

Approx. 3 lb (1½ kg) loin of pork	Pinch of pepper
Pinch of sage	Pinch of dry mustard
Pinch of salt	1 med. sized onion, chopped finely

Score the skin of the pork. Mix the seasonings with the chopped onion and rub the mixture into the whole of the pork. Wrap in foil and roast in a hot oven for one and a half hours. Remove the foil and baste the pork. Return to the oven for another thirty minutes to brown the crackling. Serve with apple sauce.

Poor Man's Goose

1 lb (450 gm) pork
2 lb (900 gm) potatoes
1 teaspn dried sage

1 teacupful stock
Pepper and salt
1 teaspn lemon juice

Parboil the potatoes and cut them into slices about quarter-inch thick. Slice the pork thinly.

Put a layer of potatoes at the bottom of a greased pie dish and top them with a layer of pork slices. Season with salt and pepper and sprinkle with the sage. Continue with alternate layers of potatoes and pork slices until the dish is full, finishing off with a layer of potatoes. Add the lemon juice to the stock and pour over the potatoes. Cover with a greased paper and bake for one and a half hours in a moderate oven. Twenty minutes before serving remove the paper and allow the potatoes to brown. Serve with apple sauce.

Ham and Pineapple

Per person:
1 slice raw ham about ½ in. (1 cm) thick

1 slice pineapple
1 teaspn brown sugar
1 tablespn cooking oil

Put the pineapple slices in the lightly greased grill pan and place the ham slices on the grid. Brush the ham with the oil and grill, turning twice until nicely cooked, allowing the juices to drip over the pineapple. Remove the ham and keep hot. Sprinkle the pineapple with the sugar and allow it to melt under the grill.

Serve fried mushrooms, peas and mashed potatoes with this dish.

Pot Roasted Ham

1 slice ham about 1 in. (approx. 2 cm) thick
2 tablespns brown sugar
3 cooking apples
6 potatoes

Pepper
Salt if necessary
1 meat cube
½ cup water

83

Cut the fat off the ham, chop the fat into small pieces and sprinkle them over the bottom of a casserole. Lay the ham on top and sprinkle with the sugar. Peel and core the apples, slice thickly and lay them on the sugared ham. Peel the potatoes, slice thickly and cover the apples. Dust with pepper. Add the water and cover with a tight-fitting lid. Bake in a moderate oven for about one hour, inspecting it occasionally to see if more water is needed and at the same time basting the potatoes. When cooked drain off the juice and mix it with the meat cube. Serve separately as gravy.

Seville Ham

| Shank or thick piece of ham about | 2 tablespns orange marmalade |
| 2 lb (900 gm) | 1 teaspn brown sugar |

Place the ham in a saucepan, cover with cold water and bring to the boil. Simmer for forty minutes. Lift out and when cool enough to handle remove the skin. Place on a piece of foil large enough to cover the ham completely. Spread the marmalade over the fat and fold the foil loosely over the top. Put into a roasting tin and cook in the middle of a moderate oven for another thirty minutes. Uncover the ham, sprinkle with the brown sugar and return to the oven for about ten minutes to melt the sugar.

Chicken with Almonds

4 chicken portions	2 oz (50 gm) blanched, shredded
3 oz (75 gm) butter or oil	almonds
Pepper and salt	1 tablespn lemon juice

Dust the joints with salt and pepper. Melt the butter in a frying pan or grill pan and fry or grill for about eight minutes on either side, keeping the chicken well coated with fat. Large portions may need a further five minutes grilling on either side. Remove from the pan and stir in the almonds. Cook until they are golden brown. Stir in the lemon juice and pour over the chicken.

Chicken Cream

½ lb (225 gm) minced cooked chicken	2 eggs
	Salt and pepper
1 oz (25 gm) butter, softened but not melted	½ pint (300 ml) cream
	Teaspn chopped parsley

Mix together the minced chicken, butter and beaten eggs. Season with salt and pepper and stir in the cream. Mix well together. Put into a greased basin and steam for forty minutes. When cooked turn out and pour plain white sauce over it. Sprinkle with parsley and serve hot.

Chicken and Lemon Pie

1 pint (600 ml) milk	Salt and pepper
1 lemon	1 lb (450 gm) cooked chicken meat
2 oz (50 gm) butter	
2 oz (50 gm) plain flour	1 can sweet corn
½ pint (300 ml) chicken stock	½ lb (225 gm) shortcrust pastry
½ teaspn brown sugar	

Warm the milk and the rind of the lemon over gentle heat for ten minutes. Cool and discard the lemon rind. Melt the butter in a saucepan, stir in the flour and cook over low heat for one minute. Gradually add the milk and the stock while continuing to stir. Reheat and continue stirring until it comes to the boil. Cook for three minutes. Add the sugar, the juice of the lemon and season to taste. Cover and leave to cool, stirring occasionally. Cut the chicken meat into bite-sized pieces. Drain the sweet corn and add and put chicken and corn into a deep pie dish. Spoon the lemon sauce over the chicken and cover with the pastry. Brush with beaten egg or milk, make a hole in the centre and cook in a moderately hot oven for about one hour until the pastry is brown and the filling is bubbling well.

Chicken Maryland

1 young chicken	¼ pint (150 ml) cream
4 oz (100 gm) butter	2 tablspns hot water
Salt and pepper	½ pint (300 ml) giblet stock
2 tablespns flour	1 teaspn chopped parsley
¼ pint (150 ml) milk	

Wash the neck and giblets and put them into cold salted water and cook for half an hour. Strain and keep stock hot. Joint the chicken and arrange the joints in a baking dish; sprinkle with salt and pepper and dredge them with flour. Dot each joint with small pieces of butter, using two ounces out of the four ounces for this. Melt the remaining two ounces of butter in the hot water and pour around the chicken. Bake in a hot oven for about half an hour, basting it twice with the liquid during cooking. Remove the chicken joints and keep hot. Heat the milk and cream together gently (do not boil) and keep hot. Put the baking dish with the liquid over the heat (or transfer liquid to a pan), stir in the flour. Stir in gradually the hot milk and cream and the hot giblet stock. Strain this sauce round the chicken. Garnish with chopped parsley. Serve with corn fritters.

Corn Fritters

2 oz (50 gm) S.R. flour	1 egg
Salt and pepper	1 pkt frozen cooked corn
½ teaspn mushroom ketchup or	or 1 tin corn
Worcester sauce	Deep fat for frying

Sieve together the flour and seasoning, stir in the beaten egg and beat all well together. Add the ketchup or sauce and corn (drained if canned). Have ready the hot fat and drop in tablespoons of the batter. Fry until golden brown.

Chicken Pie

Remains of a cooked chicken	½ lb (225 gm) mushrooms
4 slices of bacon	1 teaspn Worcester Sauce
2 med. sized onions	½ lb (225 gm) puff pastry
1 teaspn chopped parsley	Salt and pepper

Cut the chicken into neat pieces. Fry the bacon lightly and chop roughly. Lay the chicken pieces in a pie dish and top with the bacon. Chop the onions finely and add. Sprinkle with the chopped parsley. Roughly chop the mushrooms and strew them over the top. Just cover with water or stock and sprinkle on the Worcester sauce. Season with salt and pepper and put on the puff pastry lid. Bake in a hot oven for twenty-five to thirty minutes until the pastry is golden brown.

Coq au Vin

Chicken joints	1 oz (25 gm) flour
¼ lb (100 gm) mushrooms	½ pint (300 ml) red wine
2 small onions	½ pint (300 ml) chicken stock
3 oz (75 gm) butter	Salt and pepper
¼ lb (100 gm) bacon	Pinch sweet basil
1 clove garlic	

Fry the sliced onions and mushrooms in the butter until tender and just beginning to brown. Fry the chopped bacon. Lift them out of the fat and fry the chicken joints for about ten minutes until they are golden brown. Remove from the fat.

Crush the garlic and stir it with the flour into the butter in the pan; cook for about four minutes then gradually add the stock and the wine, bringing it just to the boil and then simmering it until it becomes smooth.

Return the chicken joints, mushrooms, onion and bacon pieces to the pan. Season to taste; add the basil and simmer gently for about thirty minutes until the chicken is nice and tender.

You may prefer to use one pint of wine instead of half a pint of wine and half a pint of stock.

If you are using an old boiling fowl instead of a chicken you should simmer for about one and a half to two hours instead of thirty minutes.

Cormorant Casserole

The cormorant or shag* is a sleek black feathered seabird much esteemed in the Hebrides for its flesh. It should be hung for at least three days before cooking (the Bruachites always buried theirs) and during this time it will lose its 'marine' flavour. You must also remove the skin from the bird before cooking and this is done in much the same way as one skins a rabbit (see page 89). The flesh is dark red and is best cut in thick slices from the breast. Usually only the breast and legs are used, the rest of the carcass being discarded.

The sliced breast and the legs of a shag
2 oz (50 gm) flour
Pepper and salt
1 large onion (chopped)
2 carrots
1 pint (600 ml) vegetable stock
Bouquet garni or pinch mixed herbs
2 oz (50 gm) dripping

Melt the dripping and fry the onion without letting it brown. Remove the onion from the fat. Season the flour with the pepper and salt and dredge the meat with this. Fry for two minutes in the dripping, then turn and fry for a further two minutes. Add the vegetable stock and bring to the boil. Add the fried onion, the carrot and the bouquet garni or mixed herbs and re-boil. Test for seasoning. Transfer to a casserole and cook in a moderate oven for about one and a half hours until the flesh is tender.

*Shags are at their best in Autumn.

Roast Grouse

Ensure the grouse when you buy it is not too 'high'. If bought undressed then you pluck, singe and draw the same as you would a chicken.

1 grouse	Pinch dried savory, if available,
Salt and pepper	but do not substitute any of
Pinch cayenne	the stronger-flavoured herbs
1 slice toast	4 rashers fat bacon
1 oz (25 gm) butter	1 teaspn flour

Take the liver out of the grouse, boil it for five minutes then chop very finely, season with salt and cayenne pepper and spread it on the toast.

Season the bird inside and out with salt and pepper and put inside it the butter and the savory. Put the toast into a baking dish, lay the grouse on it with the rashers of bacon spread over the breast. Roast in a hot oven for twenty to thirty minutes according to size, basting during cooking with the bacon fat. Remove the bacon, dredge the bird lightly with the flour and return it to the oven for a few minutes until the breast is nicely brown.

Alternatively the livers can be boiled as above, chopped then mixed with the butter, one small chopped onion, seasoned with salt, pepper and nutmeg, mixed with chopped mushrooms and a tablespoon of fresh breadcrumbs and the bird stuffed with this mixture.

For the special occasion a lovely rich gravy should accompany the bird. This is made by draining the fat from the roasting tin, leaving the sediment. Into this pour a good tablespoon of brandy and set alight. Quickly stir in a quarter-pint of thin cream (150 ml). Season and stir over gentle heat until the gravy is hot but do not allow it to boil.

Rabbit

I have lived on rabbit for weeks at a time when it was the only meat available, snaring them and skinning them myself.

You will probably be fortunate enough to buy your rabbit ready skinned but in case you have to do it for yourself here is how. Since a rabbit must be gutted as soon as it is killed the belly will be open so take hold of the rabbit by the hind legs, cut the skin round the 'ankle' and peel it from the leg carefully. Once the two legs are clear of skin, grasp them in one hand and with the other hand pull the skin firmly down towards the head. It should come quite easily though these things are always more difficult to explain than to demonstrate. Cut off the head, forepaws and feet. Wash and dry the rabbit and it is ready for use.

Roast Whole Rabbit

1 rabbit
Stuffing:

4 oz (100 gm) fresh breadcrumbs	½ teaspn thyme
2 oz (50 gm) suet	Squeeze of lemon juice
1 teaspn chopped parsley	½ teaspn grated lemon rind
	Salt and pepper

If using a proprietary brand of stuffing it is advisable to use an extra ounce of suet.

½ oz (15 gm) plain flour	1 small onion, chopped
1 oz (25 gm) seasoned flour	1 bayleaf
Dripping	1 egg
1 cup (100 ml) stock	2 tablespns redcurrant jelly
6 rashers bacon	

Put the heart, liver and kidneys of the rabbit into a pan of cold water, bring to the boil and simmer for five minutes. Strain and throw away the water. Chop heart, liver and kidneys finely.

Mix together the breadcrumbs, salt, herbs, lemon juice, rind and seasoning. Add the finely chopped liver, etc.; add the beaten egg and mix well together. Stuff the rabbit with the mixture, sew up the belly flaps and truss by tying front legs to back legs. Brush with melted dripping and place three rashers of bacon on top. Roll in foil and cook in a moderate oven for about one and a half hours. Remove foil and dredge the rabbit with half an ounce of flour; baste with melted dripping and return to the oven for a further ten minutes or until nicely browned. Lay the rabbit on a dish and keep hot. Chop up the pieces of bacon which should now be crisp. Add them to the fat in the baking tin along with the chopped onion. Heat until the onion begins to brown. Stir in the seasoned flour. Mix the redcurrant jelly with the stock. Add the bayleaf and pour into the pan. Bring to the boil and keep simmering for five minutes. Strain or remove bayleaf. Pour a little over the rabbit and dish the rest up separately. Grill the remaining slices of bacon and lay them on the dish with the rabbit. Any cold rabbit remaining can be sliced and served with salad.

Rabbit Curry

1 rabbit, jointed
2 oz (50 gm) dripping
2 med. sized onions, finely chopped
1 tart apple, shredded
1 rasher bacon, chopped
2 teaspns curry powder
½ teaspn curry paste
1 tablespn chutney

1 dessertspn tomato purée
Salt and pepper
1½ oz (40 gm) flour
1 pint (600 ml) stock or water

Garnish:
1 large onion, cut into rings
Seasoned flour

Heat the dripping and fry the washed and dried rabbit joints until golden brown. Lift them out and fry the onion, apple and bacon until all are nicely brown. Add the curry powder and paste, the chutney and the tomato purée and cook for two minutes. Add the flour and stir in the stock or water. Return the pieces of rabbit to the pan, season and simmer very gently for two hours, until the rabbit is tender. Put on a dish and keep hot. Dip the onion rings in the seasoned flour and fry in hot fat until golden brown. Garnish the rabbit with the onion rings and serve with boiled rice.

Rabbit Pie

If time permits I like to cook my rabbit pies in two stages so as to ensure that the rabbit is well cooked without the pastry becoming too dry.

1 rabbit, jointed
2 rashers bacon
2 potatoes sliced thinly
Salt and pepper
¼ teaspn powdered mace

1 dessertspn flour
1 med. size chopped onion
Stock or water
1 teaspn chopped parsley
1 lb (450 gm) shortcrust pastry

Soak the rabbit joints in cold water for an hour, then dry the joints. Put the layer of sliced potatoes in the bottom of a casserole or pie dish; next put in the joints of rabbit; lay the slices of bacon over them and finish with the chopped onion.

Mix the salt, pepper and mace with the flour and dredge this over the dish. Barely cover with stock or water and sprinkle with parsley. Cover with a lid or with foil and bake in a moderate oven for about three-quarters of an hour or until the rabbit is about three parts cooked. Take out the dish and leave it to cool for some hours. Top with a thick pastry crust, brush with beaten egg. Make a hole in the middle and bake in a moderately hot oven until the pastry is golden brown.

Rabbit Fricasse

1 rabbit	$\frac{1}{2}$ pint (300 ml) stock
1 oz (25 gm) butter	1 wineglass red wine or sherry
2 tablespn salad oil	1 small onion, finely minced
Pepper, salt	$\frac{1}{4}$ lb (100 gm) button mushrooms
Small pinch powdered mace	1 tablespn chopped parsley
1 oz (25 gm) cornflour	

Prepare the rabbit as for rabbit pie. Put the oil and butter into a saucepan with the pepper, salt and mace. Melt, then put in the pieces of rabbit and cook over a fairly high heat for about ten minutes or until they are cooked, stirring frequently. Lift out the pieces. Stir the cornflour into the fat in the saucepan and add the stock while continuing to stir. Add the mushrooms and simmer for five minutes. Add the sherry or wine, the onion and the parsley and return the rabbit pieces to the pan. Heat through but do not boil again. Arrange the rabbit on a shallow dish, pour over the sauce and serve.

Rabbit Hotpot

1 rabbit	4 thin rashers bacon
3 large onions	1 teaspn flour
Salt and pepper	Pinch of dried sage

This is a really succulent hotpot. Cut the rabbit into small pieces, i.e. each leg in two pieces and the body into at least four. Toss them in seasoned flour. Slice the onions and put a layer into the bottom of a casserole; then put in a layer of rabbit; continue with alternate layers of onion and rabbit. Lay the slices of bacon over the last layer of rabbit and finish off with an onion layer sprinkled with a pinch of dried sage. Put the lid on the casserole and bake in a moderate oven for two hours (do not add stock or water) or simmer very slowly on top of the stove.

Fried Rabbit

Rabbit	Breadcrumbs
Egg	Flour

Prepare the rabbit as for rabbit pie. Toss first in seasoned flour, then dip in beaten egg and finally in the breadcrumbs. Fry in hot fat until they are nicely brown (about a quarter of an hour). Serve with brown gravy and mushrooms.

Venison

The word 'venison', even before I knew precisely what venison was, had always struck me as having a rich savoury sound. Its Biblical connotations are slightly puzzling since it is hardly likely they would be eating Highland stag in the middle of the desert, but the term probably described the flesh of the wild goat – a meat which, incidentally, I have tried and found not only meagre but rather flavourless.

Talking of stags reminds me of my friend the rector who once told me of a zealous young curate who came to his church to give the sermon one Sunday evening and took for his text the first verse of the hymn:

> As pants the hart* for cooling streams
> When heated in the chase,
> So longs my soul, O God, for Thee
> And Thy refreshing grace.

It was a well-prepared sermon, the rector said, and was

*A hart is a stag which has attained the age of five years.

delivered with great depth of feeling, but as it drew to its conclusion the young curate, intent on impressing his message on the congregation and no doubt to the delight of the youngsters present, leaned over the pulpit and declared dramatically, 'My friends, always remember, God wants your pants.'

Roast Haunch of Venison

Haunch of venison	Salt and pepper
Plain flour	Melted dripping
Water	

Venison has very little fat so when cooking one tries to preserve what little there is. Rub the haunch with melted dripping and dredge with salt and pepper. Wrap the haunch in greaseproof paper and then cover it with a stiff paste made by mixing together flour and water – the haunch should be completely covered with the paste. Cover this again with greaseproof paper. You can omit the first wrapping of paper if you think this is too much trouble. Put into a moderately hot oven and bake, allowing twenty to twenty-five minutes to the pound plus twenty-five minutes over. Test by running a skewer into the thickest part of the joint and if there is no resistance the venison is ready. It is preferable to have venison slightly underdone than slightly overdone. About half an hour before it is finished cooking, remove the paste and the wrapping paper; dredge the haunch lightly with flour, baste well with hot butter and return to the oven to brown. Serve with its own gravy and redcurrant jelly.

Venison Chops

4 chops (thin loin)	1 teaspn redcurrant jelly
2 oz (50 gm) flour	Salt and pepper
4 oz (100 gm) butter	½ wineglass red wine
1 cupful (100 ml) stock	

Season the flour and dip the chops in it. Melt the butter in a frying pan, put in the chops and brown on either side.

Transfer the chops to a covered casserole. Add the remaining flour to the butter in the pan, cook until lightly brown; stir the redcurrant jelly into the stock and add to the pan; season with salt and pepper. Remove from the heat, add the wine and pour over the chops. Bake for fifteen to twenty minutes in a moderately hot oven, the time depending on the thickness of the chops.

Venison Stew

If you have only shoulder, breast or neck of venison it is best stewed.

1 lb (450 gm) venison	1½ oz (40 gm) dripping
1½ oz (40 gm) flour	Approx. 1 pint (600 ml) stock
Salt and pepper	Bouquet garni
Pinch nutmeg	Teaspn Worcester sauce
Pinch celery salt	Glass port wine
1 onion	

Cut up the venison and toss in the flour seasoned with salt and pepper, nutmeg and celery salt. Slice the onion. Fry the onion in hot dripping until it is transparent, then add the meat and fry together until both are lightly browned. Lift the meat and onion from the fat and keep hot. Stir in the remaining flour and cook until brown, then add the stock, bouquet garni and the sauce. Bring to the boil.

Put the venison and the onions into a casserole and pour over the liquid. Cover and cook gently in a moderate oven for about two and a half to three hours. Half an hour before cooking time is up remove the bouquet garni and add the port wine.

Savoury Dishes

In the small industrial town where my father had his grocery shop the poverty was so widespread when I was a child that even those of us who were relatively comfortably off were brought up not to waste a morsel of food. It was during the years of the depression when the only dinner some children went home to was a 'chip buttie' – a couple of potato chips squashed between two slices of bread and margarine – or a 'poor man's ham sandwich', i.e. two slices of bread and margarine spread with mustard! It was a time when harassed mothers with thin hunched shoulders and strained faced averted their eyes as they hurried past the foodshops where they owed money: when the only greeting men had for one another was a despairing 'Are you workin', mate?'

I am glad to relate that the last time I visited the neighbourhood of my childhood home it had become a boom town and so blatantly prosperous that children had as much pocket money as their mothers or grannies would have had to keep a family. The most frequent questions one heard being asked were 'Are you converted?' (to North Sea gas?) and 'Are you double-glazed?'

All the same, I suspect that, like me, many of my friends cannot forget their early training in frugality. I know that the outcome of my own mother's indoctrination that all waste was wicked was that I became and still am an obsessive 'user-upper' of left-overs. Rarely do I discard the driest crust of bread (except to make a scrap pudding for my bird table in winter), the tiniest piece of bacon rind, the spoonful of vegetables left in the bottom of the dish or even the scrapings of jam from jars.

As a consequence I have at times concocted what could be described as some 'interesting' dishes. A few are best forgotten but there have been on the other hand too many occasions when the result has proved to be a really appetizing dish which alas, it has been impossible to reproduce because so many left-overs were added during its preparation that I could not recall just what ingredient or combination of ingredients might have contributed to its flavour. For me half the fun of cooking is in contriving and improvising and though I enjoy preparing an elaborate meal (even if I have to have the recipe book open beside me while doing so!) I get at least as much pleasure out of making a good, tasty and yet economical dish such as those in the following chapter, most of which can be adapted to suit the ingredients you may have at hand.

As with cooking so it is with eating: the fact that I enjoy a crown roast with all its trimmings for dinner one day does not lessen my relishing plain 'bangers-and-mash' the following day.

Bacon, Egg and Cheese Pie

8 oz (225 gm) shortcrust pastry	¼ teaspn dry mustard
2 eggs	Milk
3 oz (75 gm) bacon, chopped	1 teaspn chopped parsley
2 oz (50 gm) grated cheese	

Halve the pastry and roll out one piece to line a seven-inch pie plate. Prick well. Beat the eggs and add the chopped bacon, grated cheese and mustard. Moisten well with milk. Pour into the pastry and sprinkle with parsley. Cover with the remaining pastry and make a hole in the centre. Brush with milk and bake in a hot oven for about forty minutes until the pastry is crisp and golden brown.

Bacon, Onion and Potato Hotpot

1½ lb (700 gm) potatoes	¼ pint (150 ml) stock
4 rashers bacon	1 tablespn flour
2 med. size onions	Salt and pepper
Pinch sage	1 teaspn chopped parsley

Peel the potatoes and slice thinly. Sift together the flour, pepper and salt and stir in the sage. Peel and slice the onions and dip them into seasoned flour. Cut the rind from the bacon and fry the rind until crisp reserving any fat for greasing the casserole. Chop the bacon roughly. Put a layer of sliced potatoes in the bottom of the casserole, then a layer of onions followed by a layer of bacon. Repeat until all the ingredients are used up. The crisped bacon rinds should be added with the final layer of bacon and the whole should be topped with a good layer of potatoes. Dust lightly with salt and pepper. Add stock which should come about halfway up the sides of the casserole. Put on the lid and bake for about one and a half hours in a moderate oven. Remove the lid and return to the oven for a further twenty minutes to brown the potatoes. Sprinkle with the chopped parsley.

Bacon and Onion Roly Poly

For the pastry
½ lb (225 gm) S.R. flour
¼ lb (100 gm) shredded suet
2 oz (50 gm) fresh breadcrumbs
Pinch salt
Pinch pepper
Cold water to mix

For the filling
4–6 oz (150 gm) chopped bacon
2 med. sized onions
½ teaspn thin mustard
½ teaspn chopped parsley

Make the pastry by mixing all the dry ingredients together and adding cold water until the dough is nice and soft. Work quickly while mixing. Roll the dough into an oblong; spread very lightly with the mustard; cover with the thinly sliced onion and then with the chopped bacon; dust with a little pepper and sprinkle with the parsley. Wet the edges of the pastry and roll up, pinching the edges together firmly.

Dip a pudding cloth into boiling water and then rub plain flour into it. Wrap the roll in the cloth; tie the ends securely with string. Have ready a steamer or a pan of boiling water in which there is a plate to keep the roll off the bottom of the pan. Boil for one and a half hours or steam for two hours. Ensure that the water does not cover the roll and also that it does not go off the boil.

When cooked take off the cloth, cut into thick slices and serve hot with parsley sauce.

Birdy Pancakes

For the pancakes	For the filling
½ lb (225 gm) flour	Minced remains of cold chicken,
1 egg	turkey, etc.
1 tablespn salad oil	White sauce
Salt and pepper	1 dessertspn chopped parsley
Milk	

Sieve the flour, salt and pepper together. Make a well in the centre and beat in the egg. Add the oil and mix to a medium thick batter with milk. Put in a cool place for about one hour or longer if possible. Grease a frying pan lightly and when smoking hot put in enough batter to cover the bottom of the pan. Cook until golden brown. Turn and cook the other side.

Have ready the minced turkey or chicken mixed with a little white sauce. Spread on the pancake. Roll up and keep on a hot dish covered with a linen cloth until all the pancakes are cooked. Sprinkle with chopped parsley and serve hot.

Black Pudding

Black pudding is just as revolting to make as haggis and the remarks regarding cooking and eating it also apply. One has to be hungry to do both.

Stomach bag or intestines of sheep	3 teaspns pepper
1 quart (1¼ litres) sheep's blood	2 dessertspns salt
½ pint (300 ml) skimmed milk	1 teaspn dried mint
½ lb (225 gm) medium oatmeal	¼ teaspn nutmeg
½ lb (225 gm) finely chopped suet	

Wash the stomach bag or intestines very thoroughly and soak in salt water, if possible overnight.

Put the blood into a large basin; warm the milk and add. Mix in all the other ingredients and stir well. Fill the stomach bag three parts full (or the intestines), tie the top securely and put them into near boiling water. Bring to the boil and simmer for about one hour if boiling the stomach bag or half an hour if using the intestines. While they are boiling prick them occasionally with a large darning needle to let the air escape.

Blaven Roll

This makes a nice change from sausage rolls.

1 lb (450 gm) minced beef (uncooked)	2 oz (50 gm) softened butter
3 oz (75 gm) chopped ham	1 oz (25 gm) sugar
3 oz (75 gm) stoned raisins (chopped)	1 tablespn minced onion
	¾ lb (350 gm) shortcrust pastry

Mix together the minced beef, chopped ham, raisins, butter, sugar and onion. Roll out the pastry in an oblong and spread it with the mixture, keeping it away from the ends. Roll up and moisten the edges and pinch them well together. Brush over with milk and bake in a deep baking dish in a hot oven for the first ten minutes. Then reduce heat and continue to bake for another hour and a quarter in a slow to moderate oven. Serve hot with brown gravy.

Bubble and Squeak

So many people seem to have forgotten the habit of using up left-overs that I feel it worth while including this rather tasty dish

Left-over pieces of meat	Salt and pepper
Left-over vegetables	1 oz (25 gm) butter or fat for frying
Cold mashed potatoes	
1 onion, chopped	

Mix together the cold vegetables and the potatoes and season with salt and pepper.

Fry the meat and keep it hot: fry the onion until it is just beginning to brown and then add the cold vegetables and potato mixture. Fry for about two minutes, stirring it con-

stantly to prevent sticking. Arrange the vegetables around a
hot dish; put the meat in the centre and serve hot.

Cauliflower au Gratin

1 cauliflower
1 small onion, sliced
1½ oz (40 gm) butter
1 tablespn flour
½ pint (300 ml) milk

4 oz (100 gm) grated cheese
Salt and pepper
½ teaspn curry powder
1 egg

Boil or steam the cauliflower with the sliced onion until
tender.

Melt the butter in a saucepan; stir in the flour and cook
for one minute. Continue to stir while adding the milk. Add
all but half an ounce of the grated cheese along with the salt,
pepper and curry powder. Simmer for two minutes. Beat in
the egg and remove from the heat. Arrange the cauliflower
in a deep pie dish, pour over the sauce and sprinkle with the
remainder of the cheese. Brown in the oven or under a grill
and serve hot.

Cheese Balls

4 oz (100 gm) S.R. flour
1 oz (25 gm) soya flour
¼ teaspn salt
Shake of pepper

¼ teaspn dry mustard
3 oz (75 gm) butter or cooking fat
3 oz (75 gm) cheese, grated

Sieve the flour, soya flour, salt, pepper and mustard together.
Rub in the fat and add the cheese. With the hands work into
small balls about the size of a large marble and bake in a
moderately hot oven until golden brown – about fifteen to
twenty minutes.

Cheese Omelette

2 eggs
Pinch salt and pepper
1 tablespn cold water

1½ oz (40 gm) grated cheese
1 teaspn chopped parsley

Beat together lightly the eggs, salt, pepper and water. Lightly grease an omelette pan and make it hot. Pour in the mixture and with a palette knife keep drawing away the omelette from the sides of the pan and tilting the pan so that the uncooked egg runs into the bare spaces. Continue to do this until the omelette is quite set. Sprinkle over one ounce of the grated cheese and fold the omelette over. Lift it out on to a hot plate and sprinkle the remaining cheese over. Decorate with chopped parsley and serve immediately.

Cheese and Onion Batter

¼ lb (100 gm) flour
Salt and pepper
1 egg
½ pint (300 ml) milk

2 large onions (chopped finely)
4 oz (100 gm) grated cheese
Pinch mixed herbs

Sieve the flour, pepper and salt into a basin and beat in the egg. Add the milk and beat again. Set aside in a cold place for at least one hour.

Put the onions into a well-greased deep pie dish; sprinkle over the grated cheese. Beat the herbs into the batter and continue beating for another minute or two. Pour over the onion and cheese and bake in a hot oven for about twenty-five minutes until the batter is golden brown and set.

Cheese Pudding

½ oz (15 gm) butter
½ pint (300 ml) milk
2 oz (50 gm) fine breadcrumbs
2 oz (50 gm) grated cheese

Pinch salt
Saltspoon dry mustard
1 egg

Melt the butter in a pan and add the milk. Heat but do not boil. Mix together the breadcrumbs, grated cheese and salt and dry mustard. Pour the hot milk and butter over the dry ingredients and add the beaten yolk of egg. Whip the white of egg until stiff and fold in lightly. Pour into a well-greased pie dish, leave to stand for thirty minutes. Bake in a moderate oven for half to three-quarters of an hour until firm and golden brown.

Cream and Bacon Flan

For the pastry

8 oz (225 gm) plain flour
Pinch salt
4 oz (100 gm) softened (but not
  melted) butter
1 egg
Cold water to mix

Filling

6 rashers smoked bacon
3 eggs
Pepper and salt
¼ pint (150 ml) fresh cream
¼ pint (150 ml) sour cream
1 teaspn chopped parsley

Sift together the flour and salt. Rub in the butter and work in the yolk of the egg with the tips of the fingers, gradually adding enough cold water to make a good workable dough. Leave for an hour in a refrigerator. Use the dough to line a large flan tin.

Lightly fry the bacon. Cut it into small pieces and place the bacon on the pastry. Beat the three eggs plus the white remaining from the egg used for the pastry. Add pepper and salt and stir in the fresh cream. Now very carefully stir in the sour cream. Pour over the bacon in the pastry case and bake in a hot oven for about thirty minutes. Decorate with chopped parsley before serving.

Cuillin Potatoes

1 lb (450 gm) cooked potatoes
2 slices bacon
6 oz (175 gm) mushrooms,
  chopped
1 tablespn chopped parsley
1 tablespn chopped onion

2 oz (50 gm) butter
½ cup (50 ml) milk or 2 tablespns
  cream
2 eggs
Salt and pepper

Sieve the potatoes. Fry the bacon until crisp. Chop and add to the potatoes along with the washed mushrooms, the parsley and the onion. Melt the butter and add along with the milk or cream. Beat the eggs and add. Season to taste and beat again. Put into a well-buttered pie dish and bake in a moderate oven for thirty to forty minutes.

Curried Eggs

4 hard-boiled eggs
2 med. sized onions
2 small cooking apples
1 oz (25 gm) dripping or butter
1 teaspn cooking oil
1 dessertspn curry powder

½ teaspn curry paste
1 dessertspn cornflour
½ pint (300 ml) stock
1 dessertspn sweet chutney
1 dessertspn tomato purée
1 teaspn brown sugar

Peel and chop the onions and apples. Melt dripping or butter in a pan with the oil; put in the onions and apples and cook gently until the onions begin to turn brown. Stir in the curry powder and the paste and cook for a few minutes, stirring occasionally. Stir in the cornflour and cook for one minute, stirring all the time. Add the stock and bring to the boil, still stirring. Add the chutney, brown sugar and tomato purée. Cover and simmer gently for about half an hour.

Cut the eggs into halves. Arrange neatly in a dish and pour over the sauce. Serve with hot buttered toast.

Egg Cocottes

1 oz (25 gm) butter
3 slices tomato
3 eggs

Pepper and salt
½ teaspn chopped parsley

Butter three cocotte dishes and put a slice of tomato on the bottom of each. Break an egg into each dish, dust with pepper and salt and put a small nut of butter on top. Bake in a moderate oven for about five minutes until the egg is as firm as you like it to be. Decorate with chopped parsley and serve hot with bacon or with toast.

Egg Puffs

4 oz (100 gm) S.R. flour
Salt and pepper
4 oz (100 gm) grated cheese

4 large eggs or 5 small ones
Deep fat for frying

Sieve the flour, salt and pepper together in a basin. Add the cheese and beat in the yolks of eggs one at a time to make a smooth thick batter. Whisk the whites of the eggs stiffly and fold into the mixture. Have ready some hot deep fat and drop in spoonfuls of the batter. They should puff up and become golden brown very quickly. Drain on kitchen paper and serve immediately.

Haggis

Haggis, 'The great Chieftain of the puddin' race', as Robert Burns described it, is indeed a toothsome morsel and it is a great pity that so many English people look upon it more as a Scottish joke than as a good Scottish dish. However, since haggis is made from the stomach, lungs and other internals of a sheep it is rather a gruesome sight during certain stages of its cooking, as anyone who has witnessed the process will agree. The lung must first be heated in a pan of hot water with the trachea hanging over the side so as to allow any blood and froth to escape and the stomach bag must be cleaned and scraped and washed very thoroughly before it is used. I may say from experience that it needs a fairly robust stomach to first prepare haggis and then eat it.

If you can buy ready-cooked haggis I do strongly recommend you to try it. All you need do is to slice it and fry it in a lightly greased frying pan. If you cannot buy ready-made haggis then the following is a tasty substitute.

Haggis (Mock)

½ lb (225 gm) liver	Pinch pepper
½ lb (225 gm) minced beef	Pinch grated nutmeg
2 med. sized onions	Approx. ½ cup (50 ml) of water
6 oz (175 gm) medium oatmeal	in which liver has been boiled
6 oz (175 gm) shredded suet	Pinch of cayenne pepper
1 teaspn salt	

Boil the liver for five minutes. Drain and put aside to cool. Toast the oatmeal in a dry frying pan or in the oven until it begins to turn a pale brown. Peel and mince the onions and the liver. Mix all the ingredients together with the seasoning and stir in some of the water in which the liver has been boiled. The mixture should be thoroughly moist but not wet. Have ready a greased basin large enough to give the mixture room to swell. Cover with greaseproof paper and a cloth and boil or steam for three hours.

The traditional way to serve haggis is with mashed potatoes and turnips – 'tatties and neeps', as they are called in Scotland – and to give the meal a truly Scottish flavour you should serve a glass of whisky along with it.

I like to let the mock haggis go cold and then slice it and heat it through in a frying pan (without fat) until golden brown on both sides. This way it is very good with poached eggs and even with chips.

Note: If your mince looks to be on the fatty side then cut down the quantity of suet to four ounces (100 gm).

Harvest Sausage

1 oz (25 gm) flour	1 lb (450 gm) potatoes
Salt and pepper	1 apple
½ lb (225 gm) sausage meat	1 onion
½ lb (225 gm) lean bacon	1 teaspn mixed herbs
½ lb (225 gm) tomatoes	Stock

Sieve together the flour, salt and pepper.

Cut the sausage meat and the lean bacon into bite-sized pieces and dip in the seasoned flour. Slice the tomatoes. Peel and slice the potatoes and the onion. Grease a casserole with dripping and put in a layer of potatoes; season lightly. Add a layer of the mixed sausage meat and bacon and then a layer of a mixture of apple, onion and tomato. Sprinkle over the mixed herbs and top with a layer of potato. Dust with pepper and salt. Half fill the casserole with stock or water. Put the lid on the casserole and cook in a moderate oven for two hours. Remove the lid twenty minutes before cooking time is up to crisp the potatoes.

Kyle Sausage Hotpot

2 lb (900 gm) potatoes
1 oz (25 gm) dripping
1 tablespn chopped onion
1 oz (25 gm) fine oatmeal
¾ pint (450 ml) vegetable stock

1 teaspn Marmite
2 tablespns chopped parsley
Salt and pepper
1 lb (450 gm) sausages

Boil or steam the potatoes in their jackets. Peel and slice them about half-inch thick. Melt the dripping in a saucepan, add the onion and oatmeal and fry until golden brown. Pour in the stock and stir with a wooden spoon until it boils. Add the Marmite and stir until dissolved. Add the parsley and seasonings and simmer for three minutes. Arrange the sliced potatoes in a well-greased pie dish. Pour the sauce over them and put into the oven to heat through – about fifteen to twenty minutes. Meantime grill the sausages. Arrange on top of the potatoes and sauce and serve hot.

Macaroni Cheese

¾ pint (450 ml) boiling water
  (approx.)
2 oz. (50 gm) macaroni
1 med. size onion (chopped)
1 oz (25 gm) butter
1 oz (25 gm) flour
¾ pint (450 ml) milk

1 teaspn Worcester sauce
½ teaspn made mustard
Salt and pepper
4 oz (100 gm) grated cheese
1 teaspn Parmesan cheese
1 egg

Cook the macaroni and onion in fast-boiling water to which a teaspoon salt has been added. When soft drain and keep hot.

Melt the butter in a saucepan, stir in the flour and cook for one minute. Add the milk and bring to the boil. Add the salt and pepper, the mustard and the sauce. Simmer for two minutes. Remove from the heat and stir in the grated cheese, macaroni and onion. Blend well. Add the beaten egg. Turn the mixture into a greased pie dish and sprinkle with Parmesan cheese. Brown under a grill or in a hot oven.

I sometimes add a quarter of a teaspoon of curry powder to the sauce mixture before adding the grated cheese.

Meat and Potato Wads

½ lb (225 gm) mashed potatoes
Salt and pepper
2 oz (50 gm) melted butter

S.R. flour
½ lb (225 gm) cold minced meat

Mix the potatoes with the salt and pepper and the melted butter. Work in sufficient flour to make a fairly stiff paste. Roll out and cut into oblongs about four inches by three inches. Put minced meat on one half of the paste and fold over the other half, moistening the edges and pinching them together. Brush over with milk and bake in a hot oven until nicely browned. Serve hot with a good brown gravy.

In Bruach there grew a wide variety of mushrooms and when I had identified them as being edible I used fairy ring, parasol, boletus and beefsteak mushrooms in addition to the ordinary mushrooms which grew abundantly on the moors. I was never quite certain that I had identified the beefsteak mushroom correctly since it is reputed to grow on tree trunks and there were virtually no suitable trees in Bruach. The beefsteak mushrooms I used grew on the old thatched roofs of cottages and byres. I never came to any harm through eating them so I can only assume they were edible but even so I think it is a good idea to have any wild mushrooms you have gathered identified by an expert since I understand the poisonous varieties are the ones most easily confused with the ordinary field mushroom.

Here is a recipe for using mushrooms as a breakfast or high tea dish.

Mushroom Scramble

½ lb (225 gm) mushrooms
1 oz (25 gm) butter
1 tablespn flour
½ pt (300 ml) milk

Salt and pepper
½ teaspn sweet basil
3 eggs

Wash and chop up the mushrooms roughly. Drain on a cloth. Melt the butter and stir in the flour. Cook gently until just beginning to brown. Stir in the milk, salt, pepper and sweet basil. Add the chopped mushrooms and simmer for three minutes. Add the beaten eggs and re-heat but do not boil. Serve on hot buttered toast. Beetroot makes a very good accompaniment to this dish.

Oatmeal, Cheese and Tomato Pie

The tomato pulp referred to in the recipe can be made by putting a can of tomatoes through a sieve or by diluting tomato purée with a little milk or water.

6 oz (175 gm) shortcrust pastry	⅓ pint (200 ml) tomato pulp
1 oz (25 gm) dripping or butter	Salt and pepper
1 onion	¼ teaspn dry mustard
1 slice chopped bacon (preferably smoked)	Small pinch sweet basil
1½ oz (40 gm) medium oatmeal	4 oz (100 gm) grated cheese
	1 dessertspn chopped parsley

Make the pastry and line either patty pans or one pie dish.

Melt the dripping or butter. Add the chopped bacon and onion. Fry for one minute. Stir in the oatmeal, using a wooden spoon and gradually add the tomato pulp. Continue cooking and stirring until the mixture is of a creamy consistency (about six minutes). Add the seasonings and all but one ounce of the grated cheese. Pour the mixture into the pastry case, sprinkle over the remaining one ounce of cheese and bake in a hot oven for twenty minutes. Garnish with the chopped parsley and serve hot.

The bacon may be omitted if a vegetarian dish is preferred.

I do admit not only to liking the flavour of onions but also to a belief in their germ-killing qualities. Whenever I suspect I am in for a dose of the cold I take a salad composed mainly of raw onion and parsley chopped and mixed together (this also makes a nice 'hot' sandwich filling) or else I contrive to cook a dish which contains a large proportion of onion. More often than not the signs of cold will have disappeared within a few hours.

I believe it used to be the custom to keep half a raw onion on a saucer – cut side up – in the kitchen to catch any stray germs which might be lurking around, the idea being that germs cannot live on onion juice. The onion was always discarded after a few days and replaced with a fresh-cut half.

Peeling onions can be a tearful business I know and being one of those people who can produce tears almost at the bat of an eyelid I have been given much advice on how best to stem them. The most effective way I have found so far is to grip a pin between my teeth keeping the lips tight closed while peeling. It works very well so long as one doesn't forget the pin is there!

Onions au Gratin

2 large onions	4 oz (100 gm) breadcrumbs
Salt and pepper	1 oz (25 gm) butter
5 oz (150 gm) grated cheese	Pinch mixed herbs

Slice the onions and put a layer of them into the bottom of a well-greased pie dish. Sprinkle with pepper and salt. Add a layer of cheese and then a layer of breadcrumbs. Repeat until all but one ounce of the cheese and one ounce of the breadcrumbs are used up. Sprinkle the herbs over the last layer of onion and sprinkle over the remaining breadcrumbs. Dot with the butter and bake in a moderate oven for about an hour or until the onions are quite soft. Sprinkle with the remaining cheese and either return to the oven or put under a grill to brown. Serve hot.

Stuffed Baked Onions

4 large onions	Salt and pepper
1 oz (25 gm) oatmeal	1 oz (25 gm) dripping
½ pint (300 ml) water	Pinch sage
4 oz (100 gm) cheese, grated	1 tablespn chopped parsley

Peel the onions and boil in salted water for fifteen to twenty minutes. Meanwhile cook the oatmeal in the water until it becomes thick and porridgy. Add three ounces (75 gm) of the cheese and season well with salt and pepper. Remove the onions from the water and scoop out the centres. Chop

113

the centres and add them to the oatmeal mixture. Fill the onions with this. Put the dripping into a roasting tin and heat it. Put in the onions and baste well with the hot dripping. Sprinkle with the chopped sage and bake in a hot oven for three-quarters of an hour. Five minutes before cooking time is complete remove the dish from the oven and sprinkle over the remaining cheese. Put back into the oven until it is melted. Decorate with chopped parsley and serve hot.

Potato Boulettes

½ lb (225 gm) mashed potatoes	Salt and pepper
1 oz (25 gm) melted butter	Deep fat for frying
2 eggs	

Mix the potatoes with the butter and beat in the yolks of the eggs. Season with salt and pepper. Whisk the whites of the eggs until stiff and fold them into the potatoes, mixing quickly and thoroughly. Have ready some deep boiling fat and drop the potato mixture into it a spoonful at a time. They should quickly swell to double their size. Fry until light golden brown, drain on kitchen paper and serve hot.

These boulettes make a nice accompaniment to fish or cheese dishes.

Quick Pizza

Dough	*Filling*
4 oz (100 gm) S.R. flour	1 oz (25 gm) butter
½ teaspn salt	¼ lb (100 gm) streaky bacon
2½ oz (65 gm) melted butter	1 small onion, chopped
Cold water to mix	1 apple, peeled and chopped
1 tablespn olive oil	1 small tin tomatoes
	Pinch mixed herbs
	Pinch black pepper
	1 oz (25 gm) grated cheese

Sieve the flour and salt into a basin and stir in one table-spoonful of melted butter. Mix quickly with enough cold water to make a soft dough. Roll out on a floured board to a circle a little less than the frying pan you are using. Heat the remaining butter in the frying pan along with the oil. Carefully put in the dough and cook over a medium heat for about four minutes or until the underneath is a nice golden brown. Turn carefully and spread the cooked side with the filling. Cook for another four minutes. Sprinkle with grated cheese and brown under the grill or in the oven.

Filling: Melt the butter in a pan. Remove the rind from the bacon. Chop and fry the bacon in the butter. Add the onion and apple and fry until soft. Add the tomato pulp, herbs, pepper and cook gently for five minutes, mixing well with a wooden spoon. Boil for two minutes. It is now ready to spread on the pizza in the pan.

Rhuna Hash

1½ oz (40 gm) butter or dripping	Pinch powdered sage
1 large onion	Salt and pepper
1 large cooking apple	
1 lb (450 gm) mashed potatoes	*Batter*
1 dessertspn tomato purée (or small tin tomatoes)	4 ozs (100 gm) flour
	1 egg
½ teacup (50 ml) milk	Pinch salt and pepper
1 lb (450 gm) pork sausages	¼ pint (150 ml) milk

Melt 1 oz (25 gm) of the dripping or butter in a pan. Slice the onion into rings and fry. Peel and slice the apple, add to the onion and fry until golden brown. Stir in the tomato purée or tinned tomatoes.

Heat the milk with the remainder of the dripping or butter and stir into the mashed potatoes. Season to taste.

Grill or fry the sausages (having pricked them well) for two or three minutes until the skins just begin to brown.

Put half the potatoes in the bottom of a greased casserole and sprinkle them with the sage. Put in the fried onion, apple and tomato mixture. Top with the sausages and cover with the remaining potato.

Make the batter by beating the egg and milk into the seasoned flour. Pour over the potato and bake in a moderate oven for about thirty minutes or until the batter is nicely browned.

Risotto

1 teacup (225 gm) long grain rice	1 oz (25 gm) flaked almonds
2 oz (50 gm) butter	1 pint (600 ml) stock or water
1 small onion, chopped	Salt and pepper
1 red or green pepper, chopped	4 oz (100 gm) grated cheese
1 teaspn tomato juice	1 tablespn chopped chives

Wash and dry the rice. Melt the butter in a saucepan and fry the chopped onion until lightly browned. Add the rice and the pepper and fry until the rice is nicely brown. Add the tomato purée, flaked almonds and the stock or water. Season to taste and boil rapidly for ten minutes. Reduce heat and simmer slowly until all the liquid has been absorbed. Stir in the cheese and the chives. Re-season if necessary and serve hot.

Sausage Casserole

2 onions	4 tomatoes (skinned)
Salt and pepper	Pinch mixed herbs
3 cooking apples	1 lb (450 gm) sausages
1 teaspn brown sugar	

Slice the onions thinly and lay them in a baking dish. Dust with salt and pepper. Core and slice the apples into rings and lay them on top of the onion. Sprinkle with brown sugar. Slice the tomatoes and lay on top of the apples. Dust with salt and pepper and sprinkle over the mixed herbs. Prick the sausages and arrange on top. Bake in a moderately hot oven for about twenty minutes, turning the sausages halfway. Drain away the fat and serve hot with mashed potatoes.

Sausage and Tomato Pie

2 oz (50 gm) butter	Salt and pepper
1 small onion, peeled and sliced	¼ pint (150 ml) stock
1 lb (450 gm) pork sausages	1 lb (450 gm) cooked and
2 large tomatoes	mashed potatoes

Melt half the butter in a saucepan and add the onion. Fry until golden brown. Prick the sausages and grill or fry them.

When cooked remove the skins and cut the sausages in half lengthwise. Lay half the sausages in the bottom of a pie dish and cover with the onion. Slice the tomatoes and lay on top. Dust with salt and pepper. Arrange the remaining sausages over the tomatoes and add the stock. Cover with a thick layer of mashed potato. Smooth down and dot with the remaining butter. Brown in a hot oven or under a grill.

Savoury Sausage Flan

1 lb (450 gm) sausage meat	1 small onion, chopped
2 eggs	1 tablespn chopped parsley
½ pint (300 ml) milk	Salt and pepper

Use the sausage meat to line a flan ring or shallow fireproof dish, levelling it. Beat the eggs, stir in the milk and add the chopped onion, parsley and seasoning. Pour into the sausage case and bake in a moderate oven until set and the sausage meat well cooked (about half an hour). This can be eaten hot or cold.

Scottish Mealy Pudding

½ lb (225 gm) medium oatmeal	½ teaspn pepper
2 medium sized onions	¼ lb (100 gm) shredded suet
1 teaspn salt	

Mix all the ingredients together in a basin. Do not add water. Dip a cloth into boiling water and rub it well with flour. Put the mixture into the cloth and tie securely. Drop into boiling water but do not allow water to come more than two-thirds the way up the pudding. Boil for three hours, replenishing the water as it boils away. When cold, slice and fry with bacon or as an accompaniment to sausages, liver, etc.

Skirlie

2 oz (50 gm) suet (suet from the butcher is preferred to shredded suet for this recipe)	Approx. ¼ lb (100 gm) med. oatmeal
2 onions (chopped)	Pepper and salt

Chop the suet and put into a hot frying pan. When melted stir in the chopped onion and fry until brown. Stir in oatmeal until the mixture is fairly thick. Season and serve hot with mashed potatoes or with bacon.

Swedes au Gratin

1 lb (450 gm) swede	1 oz (25 gm) breadcrumbs
4 oz (100 gm) cheese, grated	Salt and pepper
Pinch nutmeg	1 oz (25 gm) butter
½ pint (300 ml) milk	

Peel and cut the swedes into wafer-thin slices. Place a layer of the swede in a greased casserole, dust with salt and pepper, sprinkle with grated cheese and a little of the nutmeg. Repeat until all the swede and all but one ounce of the cheese is used up. Barely cover the swede with milk. Mix the remaining one ounce of cheese with the breadcrumbs and sprinkle them over the top. Dot with the butter and bake in a moderate oven for one hour or until the swedes are tender and the top is nicely browned. Serve with bacon and mashed potatoes.

As a small child I loved Sunday mornings because on Sundays my father always got up and cooked the breakfast. While Mother enjoyed an extra hour in bed Father used to light the fire in the kitchen range, get out the old Dutch oven and thread the slices of bacon on to the hooks. Mother always refused to use the Dutch oven, regarding it as too antiquated. She cooked bacon on the gas stove in the scullery, but Father maintained that bacon cooked in a Dutch oven was far superior in flavour to that fried in a pan, so when it was his turn to cook breakfast he ensured it was cooked the way he liked it. It was my job to watch the bacon and call out when it looked done and, lying on the old peg rug in front of the fire, I found it fascinating to actually watch food cooking. Indeed I became so absorbed in seeing the bacon first spit, then sizzle and then gradually curl that I didn't in the least mind knowing that the job was given me only to keep me out of the way during the rest of the breakfast preparations.

The only time Father fried bacon in a frying pan was when we had 'tomato bacon toast'. It was his name for the dish and it was easily my favourite breakfast. I still enjoy it today. Here is the recipe:

Tomato Bacon Toast

Bacon rashers (my own choice is smoked bacon)
1 tin tomatoes

Slices of white bread about $\frac{1}{2}$ to $\frac{3}{4}$ in. thick ($1\frac{1}{2}$ cm)
Salt and pepper

Fry the slices of bacon in the frying pan and when they are sufficiently cooked lift them out and keep them hot. Into the pan tip the can of tomatoes and squash them with either a fish slice or a wooden spoon as they come up to the boil. Add salt and pepper to taste. Put in the slices of bread, cook quickly and then turn them over. The slices should be thoroughly soaked with tomato but should not be allowed to get too soft to stay whole. Lift them on to a warmed plate and top with slices of bacon. Any tomato remaining in the pan should be poured over as sauce.

Puddings and Sweets

In Bruach we had no resident bull and had to rely on the Department of Agriculture to loan us one of their animals. Since Department bulls are of high pedigree and therefore precious and since winter grazing in Bruach was exceedingly sparse the village was allowed to keep the bull only during the summer months, i.e. it would arrive towards the end of May when it would be put to roam with the cows on the hill until October when, having done its stint, it would be taken away, presumably to recuperate. As most of the crofters had only one or two cows, the consequence of the bull's brief sojourn was that during the winter months every cow in the village was, or should have been, in calf, which meant there were no cows to provide milk – not even enough for a cup of tea at times and in those days unless you could take your tea with evaporated or condensed milk you either went without or you drank it black while you dreamed of summer calvings when there would be so much milk you would be feeding it to the hens by the bowlful.

Of course, no milk meant none for cooking, so one had to devise puddings and sweets which required no milk either in their preparation or in the sauce which should accompany them. Apart from pastries and steamed puddings the choice at first appears limited but in case of a milk shortage or of the more likely event of your having to cater for someone who does not like milk it is as well to point out that there are delicious alternatives. Lemon cream without cream is one or pineapple upside-down pudding if you want something more substantial.

Apple Cheesey

2 lb (900 gm) cooking apples	2 eggs
4 oz (100 gm) brown sugar	6 digestive biscuits
2 oz (50 gm) butter	4 ginger biscuits
1 lemon	2 tablespns castor sugar

Peel and slice the cooking apples. Cook to a pulp with a little water and beat with a wooden spoon. Stir in the brown sugar, butter and the juice and grated rind of the lemon. Cook for another two minutes. Cool and beat in the yolks of the eggs.

Line the bottom of a pie dish with the digestive biscuits and arrange the ginger biscuits on top. Pour in the apple mixture carefully and leave for twenty minutes to half an hour until the apple has soaked into the biscuits. Whisk the whites of eggs until stiff. Add the castor sugar and whisk again until stiff. Pile on top of the apple mixture and cook in a cool oven for about forty minutes to crisp the meringue. Serve with fresh cream.

Apple Crumble

1 lb (450 gm) cooking apples	4 ozs (100 gm) flour
4 oz (100 gm) sugar	2 ozs (50 gm) butter

Peel and core the apples and cook until tender. Add two ounces of the sugar and beat altogether with a wooden spoon. Grease a pie dish and put in the apple pulp.

Rub the butter into the flour until it is like fine breadcrumbs. Add the remaining two ounces of sugar and mix well. Sprinkle this mixture over the top of the apples but do not press down. Cook in a moderate oven for about half an hour until the top turns pale golden brown.

Apple Flan

6 oz (175 gm) shortcrust pastry	1 teaspn castor sugar
1½ lb (½ kg) cooking apples	Lemon curd
¼ lb (100 gm) gran. sugar	

Line the flan dish with the pastry.

Peel and slice all but two of the apples and stew them with the granulated sugar to a pulp. Leave to get quite cold. Pour into the pastry case. Peel, core and slice the remaining two apples into rings and arrange them on top of the apple pulp. Sift the castor sugar over them and bake in a moderate oven for about thirty minutes. Take out and spread with warmed lemon curd. Serve hot or cold.

Apple Pancake

4 large eating apples	¼ pint (150 ml) milk
2 oz (50 gm) butter	Pinch cinnamon
4 eggs	1 oz (25 gm) castor sugar

Peel and core the apples and slice them into rings about a quarter of an inch thick. Heat the butter in a frying pan and fry the rings until they are brown on one side. Turn over and lightly brown the other side. Beat the eggs, add the milk and cinnamon and beat together. Pour over the apples in the pan and fry until the underneath is a nice golden brown. Turn upside down on a warm dish. Sift the castor sugar over and serve immediately.

Apple Pie

¾ lb (350 gm) shortcrust or rough puff pastry	2 oz (50 gm) gran. sugar (or more to taste)
1 lb (450 gm) cooking apples	1 tablespn castor sugar
1 lemon	

Line a pie dish with half the pastry.

Peel and core the apples and put the skins and the cores into a pan with the rind and juice (but not the white pith) of the lemon. Add just enough water to cover and simmer for ten minutes. Cool. Meanwhile slice the apples and fill the pastry case, sprinkling them well with granulated sugar. Strain the liquid from the pan over them and cover with the pastry lid. Bake in a hot oven for about forty minutes until pastry is cooked and golden brown. Dust with the castor sugar and serve hot or cold with whipped cream or custard.

Two or three cloves may be added to the pan when boiling the peel and cores.

1 oz (25 gm) stale cake or biscuit crumbs	1 lemon
3 large cooking apples	3 oz (75 gm) castor sugar
	1 egg

Grease a pie dish and sprinkle in the cake crumbs.

Peel and slice the apples and cook slowly with the sugar and the juice and grated rind of the lemon. Stir with a wooden spoon until light and fluffy. There should be no lumps. Add the beaten egg yolk and mix well. Beat the white of the egg until stiff and fold into the mixture. Put into the pie dish on top of the crumbs and bake in a moderate oven until nicely set and browned – twenty to thirty minutes. Serve with fresh cream.

Here is a favourite pudding – I am constantly being asked for the recipe:

Ballyre Fudge Pudding

7 oz (200 gm) butter	2 oz (50 gm) gran. sugar
8 oz (225 gm) brown sugar	⅔ cupful (75 ml) cold water
1 lb (450 gm) flour	1 egg
1 teaspn salt	6 oz (175 gm) raisins or mixture
6 teaspns baking powder	of sultanas, dates and raisins
2 oz (50 gm) lard or cooking fat	2 teaspns cinnamon

Beat six ounces (175 gm) of the butter with six ounces (175 gm) of the brown sugar until creamy and spread this mixture over the bottom and sides of a strong meat tin or pyrex dish approximately twelve inches (30 cm) by nine inches (23 cm). Put aside until the next stage is completed.

Sieve together the flour, salt and baking powder. Rub in the lard or cooking fat lightly and stir in the granulated sugar. Add the water to the beaten egg and stir slowly into the flour and fat. Mix well. Roll out the dough on a well-floured board to a thickness of about a quarter of an inch ($\frac{1}{2}$ cm) and in an oblong shape. Soften, but do not melt, one ounce (25 gm) of the butter and spread the dough with this. Now sprinkle thickly over this the fruit, cinnamon and all but about one dessertspoonful of the brown sugar. Roll up as a Swiss roll, moistening the edges and pinching them well together. Cut into slices about one and a half inch (3 cm) thick and place in the meat tin on the butter and sugar mixture. The two ends should be placed cut side uppermost. Leave in a cool place for about ten minutes and then bake in a hot oven for twenty to twenty-five minutes until well risen and golden brown. Turn out upside down on to a large shallow dish immediately it comes out of the oven. Sprinkle with the remaining brown sugar and serve hot or cold with butterscotch (page 192) or caramel brandy sauce (page 193). I prefer the latter.

Banana Pudding

2 oz (50 gm) butter	1 lemon
2 oz (50 gm) cakecrumbs	Pinch cinnamon
4 large bananas	Glacé cherries for decoration
2 oz (50 gm) sugar	

Use some of the butter to well grease a pie dish. Coat the dish with a quarter of the cakecrumbs. Mash the bananas with the sugar, grated rind and juice of the lemon and the cinnamon. Put a third of the mashed banana into the pie dish on top of the crumbs and cover with another layer of crumbs. Dot with small pieces of butter. Continue with the banana and cakecrumbs until the dish is full, finishing with a layer of crumbs well dotted with butter. Bake in a moderate oven for thirty to forty minutes and when cooked decorate with the glacé cherries.

Banana Supreme

6 bananas	1 wineglass rum
4 oz (100 gm) Demerara sugar	Fan wafers or sponge fingers
1 oz (25 gm) butter	

Peel the bananas and slice in half lengthwise. Coat liberally with the sugar. Well butter a fireproof dish and lay the bananas in this. Pour over the rum and sprinkle over the rest

of the sugar. Dot with small shavings of butter, cover and
bake in a hot oven for about twenty to twenty-five minutes.
Serve with fan wafers or sponge fingers.

Bread-and-butter Pudding

3 thin slices bread and butter	½ pint (300 ml) milk
2 oz (50 gm) sultanas	2 eggs
1 oz (25 gm) sugar	1 oz (25 gm) brown sugar
¼ teaspn cinnamon	

Cut the bread and butter into neat strips and lay them in
a buttered pie dish, buttered side up. Sprinkle each layer
with sultanas, sugar and cinnamon. Heat the milk and add
to the beaten egg. Pour on to the bread and butter and stand
for about an hour or until the bread has swelled. Bake in a
moderate oven for about half an hour until set and lightly
browned. Take out sprinkle with the brown sugar and return
to the oven for three minutes.

Bruach Cloth Dumpling

½ lb (225 gm) flour	2 oz (50 gm) fresh breadcrumbs
1 teaspn bicarbonate of soda	2 oz (50 gm) sultanas
¾ teaspn cream of tartar	4 oz (100 gm) currants
Pinch pepper	2 oz (50 gm) raisins
Pinch salt	1 egg
1 teaspn mixed spice	3 tablespns black treacle
4 oz (100 gm) shredded suet	Milk to mix

Sieve the flour, bicarbonate of soda, cream of tartar, pepper,
salt and spice together into a large basin. Mix in the suet and
the breadcrumbs. Add the currants, sultanas and raisins.
Make a well in the centre and drop in the egg. Add the
treacle and mix altogether with sufficient milk to make the
mixture of a soft dropping consistency.

Have ready a pan of boiling water. Dip a clean pudding
cloth into it. Put on to a board and rub plain flour into it.
Pour the mixture on to the floured side of the cloth and draw
the cloth evenly over the top, bunching it together. Tie firmly
with string.

Put an enamel plate on the bottom of the pan of boiling water and lower the dumpling on to the plate taking care that the water does not at any time come more than halfway up the dumpling. Boil for three and a half to four hours, adding more boiling water if necessary.

When cooked lift out and peel off the floured cloth. The dumpling should have a light coloured 'skin' over a dark, fruity interior.

The dumpling is usually sliced and eaten hot or cold and it will keep for several days.

Carrageen Mould

The crofters used to gather bunches of carrageen from the shore in the spring. The carrageen was then well washed (in sea water) and spread on the grass to get the night dew. In the morning it was put into fine net and hung out to bleach for several days preferably during showery weather. When the carrageen had bleached to a pinky white it was dried in the sun and stored for winter use.

Carrageen is supposed to be very good for chest and stomach sufferers and for children.

1 oz (25 gm) dried carrageen	2 lemons ⎫ or two Seville
1 pint (600 ml) water	1 orange ⎭ oranges
6 oz (175 gm) sugar	Green colouring

Thinly pare the rind from the fruit. Put rind and carrageen into the water and boil for fifteen minutes. Strain the juice from the fruit and add the sugar. Add to the boiling liquid. Remove from heat, strain and add a few drops of green colouring. Pour into a mould and when set turn out and serve with whipped cream.

This recipe with double the amount of water makes a soothing cough cure.

Cherry and Almond Crumble

1 can cherry-pie filling	1 oz (25 gm) flaked almonds
4 oz (100 gm) plain flour	Pinch salt
2 oz (50 gm) margarine	Small pinch mace
2 oz (50 gm) castor sugar	

Sieve together the flour, salt and mace. Rub the fat into the flour until it resembles fine breadcrumbs. Stir in the sugar and add the flaked almonds. Put the cherries into a greased pie dish and sprinkle the mixture over the top. Bake in a moderate oven until the topping is golden brown (about thirty minutes). Serve with whipped cream.

Chocolat au Rhum

¾ lb (350 gm) marshmallows	Pinch salt
¾ lb (350 gm) plain chocolate	¼ pint (150 ml) cream
6 tablespns rum	1 teaspn castor sugar
6 eggs	Vanilla essence
3 oz (75 gm) butter	

Put the marshmallows into a basin and grate the chocolate over them. Add the rum and, stirring occasionally, heat the basin over a pan of hot water until the marshmallows and the chocolate are melted.

Remove from the heat and add the very lightly beaten yolks of the eggs, then the butter. Heat again over hot but not boiling water until the butter has melted. Lift the basin from the water and set aside to cool, but do not allow it to set.

Whisk the whites of the eggs with the salt until stiff, then gently fold into the cooled chocolate mixture. Put into custard glasses. Whip the cream with the castor sugar and add one or two drops of vanilla essence. Pipe the cream on to the chocolate when you are sure it is quite cold.

Christmas Pudding

My friend 'Muffet', who is a splendid cook, gave me this recipe for Christmas pudding. It has been handed down from

her grandmother via her mother and I can vouch for its
goodness.

½ lb (225 gm) sticky raisins
½ lb (225 gm) sultanas
½ lb (225 gm) currants
4 oz (100 gm) candied peel
4 oz (100 gm) chopped dates
¼ lb (100 gm) tart apple (weight
  when peeled)
2 oz (50 gm) chopped almonds
6 oz (175 gm) S.R. flour
½ teaspn salt
1 teaspn nutmeg
¼ teaspn ground ginger
½ teaspn cinnamon

¼ teaspn mace
2 oz (50 gm) ground almonds
½ lb (225 gm) shredded suet
½ lb (225 gm) brown sugar
6 oz (175 gm) fresh breadcrumbs
1 orange
1 lemon
3 eggs
1 tablespn golden syrup
¼ pint (150 ml) old ale or
  Guinness
1 wineglassful rum or sherry

Prepare all the fruit and mix with the chopped apple and
chopped almonds. Sieve together the flour, salt, nutmeg,
ginger, cinnamon and mace. Add the rest of the dry ingredients and stir in the juice of the orange and the lemon. Grate
the lemon and orange rind and add. Make a well in the
centre of the bowl and add the beaten eggs, syrup and
Guinness and the glass of rum or sherry. Mix well and set
aside covered with a cloth for twenty-four hours to ripen.
Pack into well-greased basins, cover with greaseproof paper
and foil and then with a cloth. Tie securely and boil for at
least eight hours. Ensure that there is always enough water
to come halfway up the basins. When cooked take off the
cloth, renew greaseproof paper and foil and store until
required. When ready to use boil for another hour or hour
and a half according to the size of the puddings. Serve with
brandy sauce (page 192).

Comfrey-leaf Pancakes

¼ lb (100 gm) flour
Pinch salt
1 egg

Milk to mix
Comfrey leaves

Sieve the flour and the salt together. Make a well in the
centre and drop in the yolk of the egg. Beat into the flour

along with enough milk to make a creamy consistency. Whisk the egg white until stiff and fold into the batter.

Wash and dry the comfrey leaves, dip in the batter and fry in hot fat until golden brown. Dust with sugar before serving.

Elderflower Dips

Make a batter as in the recipe for Comfrey Pancakes.

Wash and dry the sprigs of elderflowers, dip them into the batter and fry in hot fat until golden brown. Dip in sugar and eat while hot.

Cottage Pudding

Stale bread or crusts (about ¾ lb)	1 tablespn syrup
1 pint (600 ml) milk	2 eggs
2 oz (50 gm) brown sugar	½ teaspn mixed spice
2 oz (50 gm) shredded suet	2 oz (75 gm) currants

Heat the milk and stir in the bread crusts. Leave until quite soft and then mash with a fork. Add the sugar, spice, syrup and suet. Beat the eggs and add. Lastly stir in the currants. Turn the mixture into a well-buttered pie dish and bake in a moderate oven for about three-quarters of an hour. Serve with marmalade orange sauce or custard.

Daffodil Pudding

2 oz (50 gm) shredded suet	1 lemon
2 med. sized carrots	Pinch salt
2 oz (50 gm) S.R. flour	1 egg
2 oz (50 gm) breadcrumbs	Approx. ½ teacup (50 ml) milk
2 oz (50 gm) brown sugar	

Sieve the flour and salt into a basin: add the breadcrumbs. Grate the carrots and add. Stir in the sugar and suet and the finely grated rind of the lemon (no white pith). Add beaten egg along with the juice of the lemon. Mix together adding the milk a little at a time until the mixture is of a soft dropping consistency. Pour into a greased basin, cover with greaseproof paper and boil for one and a quarter hours or steam for two hours. Serve with custard sauce or with marmalade orange sauce.

Elderberry Sponge

1 lb (450 gm) ripe elderberries	12 sponge fingers or 4 sponge cakes
¼ lb (100 gm) sugar	Cream

Strip the elderberries roughly from their stalks and stew with just enough water to cover until they are soft enough to be put through a sieve. When sieved stir in the sugar and cook over gentle heat until dissolved. Put the sponge fingers, cut into halves, on the bottom and around the sides of a glass dish. Pour in the elderberry pulp and leave for at least two hours. Serve with cream.

Blackberries, blackcurrants or raspberries are also suitable for this dish. Barberries may also be used but as they are somewhat more tart they need extra sugar.

Fig Pudding

4 oz (100 gm) flour	4 oz (100 gm) sugar
Pinch salt	5 oz (150 gm) figs, chopped
1 teaspn baking powder	2 oz (50 gm) flaked almonds
Pinch mace	1 lemon
4 oz (100 gm) suet	2 eggs
4 oz (100 gm) breadcrumbs	Milk to mix

Sieve the flour, salt, baking powder and mace together into a basin. Add the suet, breadcrumbs, sugar, figs, almonds and grated rind of the lemon. Beat the eggs and add and mix with the milk to a soft dropping consistency. Stir in the juice of the lemon. Put the mixture into a greased basin, leaving room for it to rise, cover with greaseproof paper and/or foil and steam for two and a half hours. Turn out and serve with custard or with marmalade orange sauce (page 193).

French Tart

6 oz (175 gm) shortcrust pastry
2 tablespns lemon cheese

2 tablespns raspberry jam
Whipped cream

Line a pie dish with the pastry and bake 'blind' until golden brown in a hot oven. When cool, spread with a layer of lemon cheese and then with a layer of raspberry jam. Whip the cream, pipe in a circle and serve the tart cold.

Gingernut Pudding

1 pkt gingernut biscuits
¼ pint (150 ml) thick cream

2 tablespns sherry

Spread the biscuits with cream and put together to form a roll. Sprinkle with sherry and wrap in foil. Leave in a refrigerator for about two hours before serving.

Lemon Cream without Cream

2 lemons
½ pint (300 ml) water
3 eggs

2 oz (50 gm) sugar
1 oz (25 gm) ratafia biscuits

Pare the outer rinds from the lemons discarding any white pith. Squeeze out the juice from the lemons and put rind and juice into the water. Leave to soak for about two hours. Add the eggs, well beaten, and the sugar and stir over a low heat until the sugar is dissolved and the mixture begins to thicken but do not allow it to get too hot. When cool strain into glasses and decorate with ratafia biscuits.

Lemon Meringue Pie

6 oz (175 gm) shortcrust pastry
1 oz (25 gm) cornflour
½ pint (300 ml) milk
1 lemon
3 oz (75 gm) gran. sugar

½ oz (15 gm) butter
2 eggs
3 oz (75 gm) castor sugar
Whipped cream

Line a pie dish with the pastry and bake 'blind' in a hot oven for about fifteen minutes or until pale golden brown.

Blend the cornflour with a little of the milk. Boil the rest of the milk and pour on to the cornflour. Return to the pan, add the lemon juice and simmer for four to five minutes. Add the sugar, butter and the grated rind of the lemon. Cool and beat in the egg yolks one by one. Pour the mixture into the pastry case. Whisk the whites of the eggs very stiffly, add the castor sugar gradually and whisk again until stiff. Pile on top of the pie and bake in a slow oven for about half an hour until the filling is set and the meringue is nicely crisp and pale brown in colour. Serve with whipped cream.

Lemon Mousse

2 eggs, separated	Tablespn cold water
2 oz (50 gm) castor sugar	1 pkt powdered gelatine, to set
1 lemon	1 pint (600 ml)

Put egg yolks and sugar into a bowl with the grated rind of the lemon. Beat until creamy over hot but not boiling water. Remove the bowl from heat.

Squeeze lemon for juice.

Put the tablespoon of water in a very small pan, sprinkle on gelatine and put on very low heat. Stir very briskly as it warms until the gelatine is dissolved and no granules can be seen in the liquid. Beat this and the lemon juice into the egg and sugar mixture.

Beat egg whites until stiff and fold quickly and gently into the mixture. Tip at once into a soufflé dish or individual glasses, and leave to set, preferably not in a refrigerator. Serve with fresh cream.

Lemon Snow

1 pint (600 ml) milk	2 eggs
2 oz (50 gm) breadcrumbs	1 lemon
1 oz (25 gm) butter	3 tablespns castor sugar
¼ lb (100 gm) sugar (gran.)	

Warm the milk and pour over the breadcrumbs.

Beat the butter and sugar together. Add the yolks of the eggs and beat again. Add to the milk and breadcrumbs and stir in along with the grated rind and the juice of the lemon. Turn into a buttered pie dish and bake in a moderate oven until set and just beginning to brown.

Meanwhile whip the egg whites until stiff, add the castor sugar gradually and whip again until stiff. Pile on top of the pudding and put back into a cool oven until the meringue is set. Alternatively put into a moderate oven for ten minutes until the meringue is golden brown.

Marsala Custard

4 egg yolks	2 wineglasses Marsala
4 oz (100 gm) castor sugar	8 sponge fingers

Beat the egg yolks to a pale cream and mix with the sugar. Stir in the Marsala and cook in a double saucepan until the custard is thick enough to coat the back of the spoon. Pour into individual custard glasses and serve with the sponge fingers when cool.

Peach Cream

1 tin peaches	Cochineal
¼ oz (8 gm) gelatine	1 oz (25 gm) chopped cherries
1 teaspn lemon juice	1 oz (25 gm) angelica
3 oz (75 gm) castor sugar	1 oz (25 gm) chopped almonds
½ pint (300 ml) whipped cream	

Drain the peaches from the syrup and rub them through a sieve. Melt the gelatine in a little of the peach syrup. Add to the peaches along with the lemon juice and sugar. Add all but one teaspoon of the cream and colour carefully with one or two drops of cochineal. Stir until the mixture begins to set. Decorate a mould with the glacé cherries, angelica and chopped almonds and put in the mixture. When cold and quite set turn out carefully and dot with the remainder of the whipped cream.

Peach Delight

½ pint (300 ml) cream
1 oz (25 gm) icing sugar
2 oz (50 gm) grated milk
  chocolate

1 tablespn rum
Small tin peaches
1 oz (25 gm) chopped hazelnuts
Sponge fingers

Whip the cream until thick and sweeten it with the icing sugar. Stir in the chocolate and the rum carefully. Chop the peaches and fold them in lightly. Chill and garnish with hazelnuts. Serve with sponge fingers dipped in the peach syrup.

Pears with Chocolate Sauce

2 oz (50 gm) butter
3 tablespns Golden syrup
1 heaped tablespn cocoa

1 large tin pears or 4 fresh pears
  peeled and halved
Cream

Melt the butter in a saucepan but do not allow it to get hot. Stir in the syrup and cocoa and continue to stir until you have a nice smooth sauce. Drain the juice from the pears and add. Heat but do not allow the sauce to become too hot at any time.

Lay the pears in a shallow dish and pour the sauce over them. Whip the cream and put a whirl on each pear.

Pineapple Soufflé

3 oz (75 gm) butter
3 oz (75 gm) flour
½ pint (300 ml) milk
⅛ pint (75 ml) double cream
3 eggs

3 oz (75 gm) chopped pineapple
  (fresh or tinned)
¼ teaspn pineapple essence
1 tablespn sherry
Cream
Castor sugar

Melt the butter in a saucepan over gentle heat and stir in the flour. Cook for one minute but do not allow it to brown. Add the milk slowly and simmer for one minute. Remove from the heat and stir in the cream and the beaten egg yolks. Stir in the drained pineapple and the essence. Whip the whites of eggs stiffly and fold in. Turn the mixture into a greased mould and steam for one and a quarter hours. When cooked turn out and pour the sherry over it. Serve with any juice from the pineapple, whipped cream and castor sugar to taste.

Pineapple Upside-down Pudding

Topping
1 small tin pineapple
2 oz (50 gm) butter
4 oz (100 gm) soft brown sugar
Glacé cherries

Pudding mixture
3 oz (75 gm) butter or margarine

3 oz (75 gm) castor sugar
4 oz (100 gms) S.R. flour
1 egg
Pinch salt
Pinch mixed spice
Flaked almonds (optional) for decoration

Drain the pineapple from the juice. Cream the two ounces of butter and four ounces of brown sugar in a warmed basin and spread over the bottom of a seven-inch cake tin. Lay the drained pineapple slices on this and put one or two glacé cherries in the centre of each slice (one green cherry and one red cherry look nice). Grease the sides of the tin.

Cream the three ounces of butter or margarine with the castor sugar. Beat in the egg lightly. Stir in the sieved flour, salt and spice and mix to a soft dropping consistency with the juice from the pineapple. Spread this mixture over the slices and cook in a moderately hot oven for about forty minutes, lowering the heat after the first twenty minutes if the top is browning too quickly. Turn out carefully, preferably on to greaseproof paper on a wire tray. Sprinkle the top with flaked almonds if liked. This pudding may be served either hot or cold.

Prune Soufflé

½ lb (225 gm) cooked prunes
2 tablespns castor sugar

2 eggs
2 teaspns lemon juice or sherry

The prunes should be quite soft. Drain them from the syrup, remove the stones and chop the prunes. Put the sugar and egg yolks into a basin and beat them together with a wooden spoon until they are of a pale, creamy consistency. Add the lemon juice or sherry and the chopped prunes and mix well together. Beat up the whites of the eggs to a stiff froth and stir lightly into the mixture. Pour into a buttered fireproof dish and bake in a moderate oven for about fifteen minutes. Serve as soon as it is taken from the oven having first sprinkled the top lightly with a little more castor sugar.

Queen Pudding

4 oz (100 gm) fresh breadcrumbs	¼ teaspn mixed spice
¼ pint (150 ml) milk	Pinch salt
2 oz (50 gm) brown sugar	1 oz (25 gm) castor sugar
1 oz (25 gm) butter	Tablespn raspberry jam
1 egg	

Heat the milk with the butter. Put breadcrumbs into basin and mix in sugar. Pour on the milk and butter and mix with a fork. Cool for about ten minutes. Stir in beaten yolk of egg, salt and spice. Butter a soufflé dish. Put in the mixture and bake in a moderately hot oven for fifteen to twenty minutes until firm and just beginning to brown. Meanwhile whip white of egg until stiff, add castor sugar and whip again. Remove pudding from oven and spread with jam. Top with the meringue. Return to oven for about five minutes to set.

Star Queen Pudding

This is a glamorized version of Queen Pudding.

4 oz (100 gm) fresh breadcrumbs	Pinch salt
¼ pint (150 ml) milk	1 oz (25 gm) castor sugar
2 oz (50 gm) brown sugar	2 tablespns apricot jam
1 oz (25 gm) butter	1 banana
1 egg	1 tablespn brandy
¼ teaspn mixed spice	

Heat the milk with the butter. Put breadcrumbs into basin and mix in sugar. Pour on the hot milk and butter and mix with a fork. Cool for about ten minutes then stir in the beaten yolk of egg, salt, spice and brandy. Butter a soufflé dish and put in half the jam, spreading it over the bottom. Add thinly sliced banana and cover with the mixture. Bake in moderately hot oven for fifteen to twenty minutes until firm. Meanwhile whip white of egg until stiff, add castor sugar and whip again. Remove pudding from oven, spread with remaining jam and top with the meringue. Return to oven for about five minutes to set.

I am never quite sure whether the following recipe should be called a pudding or a cake since it can be eaten either hot with custard or cut into chunks and eaten cold. Black Bun is a traditional Hogmanay dish in Scotland.

Scottish Black Bun

For the paste:
½ lb (225 gm) flour
½ teaspn baking powder
Pinch salt
¼ lb (100 gm) butter
Cold water to mix

For the filling:
½ lb (225 gm) flour
½ teaspn bicarbonate of soda
Pinch pepper
¼ teaspn ground ginger

Pinch salt
Quarter teaspn mace
½ lb (225 gm) raisins
½ lb (225 gm) currants
2 oz (50 gm) almonds, ground or flaked
½ lb (225 gm) sultanas
2 oz (50 gm) shredded suet
1 tablespn castor sugar
1 tablespn black treacle
Milk to mix

Make the pastry by sieving together the flour, baking powder and salt. Rub in the butter and mix to a fairly stiff paste with the water. Roll out thinly. Line a deep cake tin with two thirds of the pastry, reserving enough to make a lid.

Sieve together the flour, baking soda, salt and spices. Add the prepared fruit, almonds, suet and sugar and mix well together. Make a well in the centre and pour in the treacle. Mix to a moist consistency with the milk. Stir well and put the mixture into the pastry case. Smooth over the top of the fruit mixture, turning in the edges of the lining pastry a little over the bun. Moisten the edges of the pastry lid and place over the mixture, pressing the edges firmly together. Prick over with a fork. Brush with milk and bake in a moderately slow oven for three to four hours.

If you can obtain buttermilk or sour milk for mixing the bun the texture will be improved.

Spotted Dick

---

6 oz (175 gm) flour
Pinch salt
1 teaspn baking powder
Pinch mixed spice
2 oz (50 gm) breadcrumbs
4 oz (100 gm) shredded suet

1 tablespn castor sugar
3 oz (75 gm) raisins
Milk to mix
1 tablespn golden syrup
1 oz (25 gm) brown sugar

Sieve the flour, salt, spice and baking powder together in a basin. Stir in the breadcrumbs and suet. Add the sugar and the raisins. Mix to a soft consistency with the milk.

In the bottom of a greased pudding basin put the golden syrup. Put in the pudding leaving room for it to rise. Cover with greaseproof paper or foil and tie with a cloth. Boil for two hours or steam for two and a half hours. Turn out on to a hot dish, sprinkle the syrupy top with brown sugar and serve with hot custard.

Strawberry Meringue Tart

For the meringue case
3 egg whites
6 oz (175 gm) castor sugar
3 level tablespns coconut

For the filling
3 egg yolks

3 oz (75 gm) castor sugar
3 tablespns lemon or orange juice

For the garnish
⅓ pint (200 ml) double cream
8 oz (225 gm) strawberries

Whisk the egg whites until stiff. Add three ounces of the sugar and whisk again. Fold in the remaining three ounces of sugar lightly. Spread the meringue on a greased pyrex plate to a thickness of a quarter-inch (½ cm) at the bottom and one inch thick (2 cm) at the edges. Sprinkle with coconut and bake in a cool oven until crisp.

Beat the yolks of the eggs in a bowl over hot, but not boiling water, with the sugar and the orange or lemon juice. When thick cool for a few minutes and fold in all but one tablespoonful of the double cream. Pour into the cooked meringue case and level with a knife. Refrigerate for twelve hours. Cover with the sliced strawberries. Whip the remaining cream and pipe in whirls over the top.

Strawberry Shortcake

For the cake	For the filling
½ lb (225 gm) flour	1 lb (450 gm) strawberries
Good pinch salt	Cream
2 teaspns baking powder	Castor sugar (approx. 3 oz)
2½ oz (65 gm) butter	(75 gm)
1 egg	
Milk to mix	

Sieve the flour, salt and baking powder into a basin. Rub in two ounces (50 gm) of the butter finely and mix to a soft dough with the egg and milk. Turn the mixture on to a board. Divide in half and knead lightly. Flatten each half into a round rather less than half inch thick. Brush each round with the remaining butter, put into two sandwich tins and bake in a hot oven until pale golden brown. When cooked remove from the tins, cool on a wire tray.

Wash and hull the strawberries and choose about ten of the best sized ones for decorating the top of the cake. Mash the rest with a silver fork adding enough castor sugar to make them sweet enough for your taste. Spread one shortcake round with cream and then top with the mashed strawberries. Place the other round on top. Spread with more whipped cream, decorate with the reserved strawberries, dredge with remaining castor sugar and pour any strawberry juice around the cake.

Syrup Sponge Pudding

4 oz (100 gm) flour	4 oz (100 gm) breadcrumbs
½ teaspn bicarbonate of soda	2 oz (50 gm) sugar
¼ teaspn salt	4 tablespns golden syrup
1 teaspn ground ginger	1 egg
4 oz (100 gm) shredded suet	Milk to mix

Sieve the flour, bicarbonate of soda, salt and ground ginger together into a basin. Add the suet, breadcrumbs and sugar. Make a well in the centre. Add three tablespoons of the golden syrup and the beaten egg and stir in with sufficient milk to make the mixture of a soft dropping consistency. Mix thoroughly. Into a greased pudding basin pour the remaining tablespoon of syrup. Put in the mixture and cover with greaseproof paper or foil, ensuring that the pudding has room to rise. Boil for two hours or steam for two and a half hours. Turn out and serve with hot custard.

There is a nice story, allegedly true, which I heard in a vicarage drawing room some years ago. It is about two golfers who were playing at a famous course in the North of England. It was early afternoon and the two golfers had indulged in a splendid lunch at the clubhouse at which one of them had succumbed to the temptation of a third helping of syrup tart or, as he called it, 'golden tart'. Perhaps as a result this man's game was that afternoon decidedly substandard. Coming up close behind them on the course were two ladies, one a strikingly attractive blonde with masses of golden hair and a curvaceous figure; the sort of woman who most men would want to impress with their prowess. But the golfer was truly off his game and when he, in full view of the blonde, sliced the ball badly he turned to his friend and said exasperatedly, 'I know what's putting me off my game. It's that damned golden tart.' Whereupon the attractive blonde walked up to him in a fury and hit him with her golf club. The golfer was flabbergasted by her action but being a thorough gentleman he only turned to her and said haughtily, 'Madam, I will accept an apology now but I will not accept one later.' Meantime his friend, divining the reason for the blonde's sudden attack, hurriedly explained the situation and the apology then being forthcoming the affair ended peaceably.

I can never make syrup tart without recalling this story.

Syrup Tart (or Golden Tart!)

6 oz (175 gm) shortcrust pastry
4 tablespns golden syrup
2 oz (50 gm) biscuit, cake or
  bread crumbs or crushed

cornflakes or a mixture of all
of them
1 teaspn lemon juice

Line a pie dish with the pastry and decorate the edges by pinching. Pour in the syrup and sprinkle over the lemon juice. Sprinkle the crumbs or cornflakes liberally over the syrup and bake in a hot oven for about fifteen minutes until the pastry is cooked and the filling is pale golden brown.

Zebra Pudding

½ lb (225 gm) breadcrumbs
2 tablespns raspberry jam

2 tablespns lemon curd
¼ pint (150 ml) thin custard

Grease a pudding basin, preferably using butter. Cover the bottom with a thick layer of breadcrumbs. Press down lightly and cover with one tablespoon of the raspberry jam. Add another layer of breadcrumbs and cover this with one tablespoon of the lemon curd. Repeat with the remaining jam and lemon curd and finish with a layer of breadcrumbs. Pour over the custard and leave to soak for about one hour. Cover with buttered paper and foil and steam for three-quarters of an hour to one hour.

Bread, With and Without Yeast

I once knew a farmer in Cheshire – a big healthy-looking man – who told me proudly he had never in his life eaten anything but bread and butter. He never ate meat or vegetables, fish or fruit, he said. Just a plate of fresh bread and butter and a couple of cups of tea for every meal. 'And make no mistake,' he asserted, 'I love it. Though I never eat anything else I still look forward to every mealtime as it comes round. There's something about the smell of a plate of bread and butter that does something to me.'

I was so awestruck that I mentioned the farmer's claim to his wife who was incidentally not only a capable cook but also one of the best cheese-makers in the county.

'Never eats anything else,' she confirmed. 'But then his mother was no cook and that's what she brought him up on. Just bread and butter. Mind you, it was good baker baked bread in those days and wholesome farm butter.'

As we stood talking we were overlooking the orchard where the trees were weighed down with an abundance of apples.

'Is he never tempted to take a piece of your own cheese or perhaps an apple from his orchard?' I asked, still reluctant to believe that a man could live an apparently hard-working and healthy life on such a diet.

'Cheese? Oh, my goodness no!' she replied. 'But I will say when the apple harvesting comes he might just once or twice take a piece of apple pie for his supper on a Sunday. Never more than twice at the most and then that's him back to bread and butter for another year.'

I regarded her with puzzled interest. How could any woman fall in love with and marry a man who lived exclusively on bread and butter? Had she hoped that married to him she could persuade him to change his diet? I ventured to put the latter question to her.

'Not really,' she admitted. 'He was thirty-five when I

married him and that's long enough for a man to get pretty set in his ways.'

My interest became tinged with admiration. I knew I could never have worked up even a passing affection for a man who ate nothing but bread-and-butter, a confession which, I suppose, reveals without doubt where my heart is situated.

I could have better understood the farmer's partiality for bread-and-butter if it had been home-made bread since to come home to the smell of fresh baked bread is, I always think, as good as coming home to a warm hug. As soon as I achieved a kitchen of my own I began to bake bread, with yeast when I could procure it, with some other raising agent when I couldn't. The resolve to bake my own bread was formed in early childhood, I think on the day I was permitted to go into Mrs Shenstone's kitchen and watch her taking her bread from the oven. There were long thin loaves, cob loaves and cottage loaves and by the time the oven was empty the kitchen table was covered with steaming, gently brown, crusty bread. As children we believed that only people who were too poor to buy bread from the baker bothered to bake their own but I know that day I envied the poor Shenstone children. It must be wonderful, I thought, to have a mother who not only baked bread but baked it so often that she herself had come to resemble one of her own cottage loaves – vast and round below the tight pulled waist-strings of her apron; small and round above and with a hairstyle that looked as if it was a deliberate repetition of the pattern – a big flat pancake crowning her head and another smaller round bun sitting plumply in the middle of it.

When I went home that evening I told my mother that I wished we were poor so that we had to have bread baked in our own oven instead of bread bought from the baker's van. Mother was cross and told me I must never, never wish to be poor but, she added, some day she would bake bread for me and let me watch her doing it. I went to bed happily. The prospect of having home-baked bread without being poor was pleasant indeed particularly when I remembered that for the Shenstone children being poor meant being dressed in 'cast-offs' and only getting an orange or an apple from Father Christmas instead of a lovely doll or toy.

I was never fortunate enough to taste any of Mrs Shenstone's bread but because it looked and smelled so good I am sure it must have been equally good to eat.

My recipe will give you a bread that not only tastes as good as it smells but also works out considerably cheaper than buying bread, and in these days of deep freezers even if your consumption of bread is small you can always economize by baking a good batch and freezing it for later use.

I hope once you have tried it, baking your own bread will become a habit and if you fear that if you continue you might, like Mrs Shenstone, come to resemble the shape of one of your loaves, well, try baking the long French type.

Irish Wholemeal Loaf

1 oz (25 gm) lard	1 teaspn cream of tartar
Milk to mix	1 teaspn bicarbonate of soda
¾ lb (350 gm) wholewheat flour	1 teaspn salt
¼ lb (100 gm) white flour	1 dessertspn syrup

Melt the lard in a saucepan but do not allow it to become hot. Add cupful of milk. Mix the dry ingredients together and make a well in the centre; add the syrup and mix in the melted lard and milk. Add more milk to bring mixture to a light consistency. Put into a greased tin and bake for one hour in a moderate oven.

Steam Bread (without yeast)

1 lb (450 gm) wholewheat flour	1 teaspn salt
1 teaspn bicarbonate of soda	1 tablespn black treacle
1 teaspn cream of tartar	Milk to mix

Mix the dry ingredients together in a bowl. Add the treacle and mix to a fairly stiff dough with the milk. Put into a greased cake tin. Cover with greaseproof paper and steam for two hours. Stand in a moderate oven for ten minutes to dry off. Slice when cold.

Wholewheat Bread

---

3 lb (1 kg) wholewheat flour
2 oz (50 gm) yeast (I use 4 oz (100 gm) because I like yeasty-tasting bread. It certainly is not necessary)
1½ tablespns sugar

1 tablespn salt
2 oz (50 gm) lard
1 tablespn malt (as used for home beer brewing)
Warm water to mix

Crumble the yeast into a warm basin and cream it with half the sugar, using a wooden spoon. Pour in half a pint of warm water and sprinkle the top with about a tablespoonful of the flour. Leave for fifteen minutes in a warm place. Meanwhile warm the bowl and flour but do not make it hot. Mix in salt and remaining sugar. Melt the lard over low heat and add a cupful of warm water. Stir in the malt, ensuring that you keep everything nicely warm. Make a well in the centre of the flour and pour in the yeast mixture which by now should be bubbling and frothing. Pour in the warm lard, malt and water and mix together, adding more warm water if necessary to make a nice pliable dough. Begin kneading it in the basin and then turn it out on to a floured board and continue kneading for as long as you have the patience to do it – up to fifteen minutes (wholewheat bread does not seem to require as much kneading as is advocated for white bread) but I usually give up after about five minutes. Put the dough back into the warm bowl and cut a cross in the top with a sharp knife. Cover and leave until it has risen to twice its size. Turn out on to a floured board and knead lightly into shape for a minute then cut again with a sharp knife into pieces weighing about three quarters of a pound each. Tuck in the ends and shape into rounds. Put on to a greased and floured baking tray or into greased and floured bread tins and put to rise for about twenty minutes in a warm place (no draughts please!). Carefully slide them into a very hot oven (475°F) trying not to shake the tins or the baking tray while you are doing it. After the first fifteen minutes lower the heat and cook for another twenty to twenty-five minutes altering the position of the loaves in the oven if they are browning unevenly.

If you are baking bigger loaves, say one and a half pounds of dough then you must increase the time for the second rising and also the time for the cooking. To test when a loaf is done turn it out and rap the bottom with the knuckles gently. It should sound hollow: or press gently with the fingers when it should spring back quickly. Bread is better slightly over-cooked than slightly under-cooked and because I like mine to be on the crusty side I turn it out of the tins and give it a further five minutes to crisp the outside all over.

Splits: Use the same bread recipe but beat up an egg and stir it into the milk and lard and water before adding it to the flour. Shape into small buns and bake on a greased and floured baking tray for about twenty minutes. Split while still warm and serve, spread lavishly with butter.

Cakes, Large and Small:
Buns and Biscuits

Nearly always on Sunday we had people come to tea and consequently a good deal of Mother's time on Saturday night was spent baking different kinds of cakes and pies. One Sunday she told me that her brother, my Uncle Jim, was to bring his new young lady to tea and, wildly excited at the prospect of meeting someone I had heard so much discussed I begged to be allowed to help set the table. Mother yielded but insisted that I was to first make sure my hands were very clean, so I pulled a chair up to the kitchen sink, filled the bowl with warm water and rubbed my hands so lavishly with soap that before I had finished the bowl was a mass of suds. When I had dried my hands I held them up for inspection.

'All right,' she said. 'Now you can put the gingerbread on this dish and take it through to the table in the living room. And be very careful,' she added, though she knew I loved gingerbread so much she hardly needed to warn me to be careful with it. 'And don't touch anything else until I come downstairs again,' she called as she disappeared. I carefully placed the gingerbread on the lace d'oyley on the dish as instructed and was on my way to the living room when through the window above the sink I noticed a cat crouched in the tree outside. Now father had taught me always to shoo cats away from the garden because he did not like them killing the birds and, thinking I would run out and shout at the cat, I put the dish and the gingerbread down on the draining board. To my horror the gingerbread slid off and fell 'plop' into the bowl of soapy water in which I had just washed my hands and which I had neglected to empty. Panic stricken I retrieved it immediately and looked around for something to wipe off the suds. The only thing within my reach was the roller towel on which we wiped our hands, so I wrapped the cake in it, patted it dry, returned it to the dish and carried it through to the living room. I was just placing it in position on the table when Father came in. I held my breath but he appeared to notice nothing amiss and praised me for helping. Mother came downstairs, glanced at the table but made no comment. My panic subsided and in the excitement of meeting Uncle Jim's young lady I temporarily forgot about the accident to the gingerbread. Panic returned when Uncle Jim held out his plate for the first slice. I watched him covertly but he did not jump up and rush out to the kitchen as I was half expecting. He ate his gingerbread and asked for another slice. And then another. I hoped he wouldn't die in agony of soapsud poisoning.

'Aren't you having any gingerbread?' mother asked, and shocked by my unprecedented refusal she gave me a probing look, no doubt suspecting that I was sickening for something.

After tea when Uncle Jim's young lady was helping Mother wash the dishes in the kitchen I heard Uncle Jim say to Father, 'There's no doubt I always enjoy a bit of our Lil's cooking. That gingerbread now; there's nobody else I know who seems to be able to bake gingerbread that eats so nice and moist as hers.' I did not look up from my illustrated bible, the only book I was allowed to have on Sundays, and I wondered if God expected me to own up. If he did, I decided, he expected too much.

There must have been more compliments in the kitchen because when Mother came back to the living room with Uncle Jim's young lady she began looking for a piece of paper and a pencil so that she could write down the gingerbread recipe for her.

The gingerbread on page 168 is nice and moist without prior immersion in soap suds!

Another of my mother's specialities was her Johnny Cake (page 167). The name Johnny Cake is, I understand, derived from 'Journey Cake', i.e. the cakes were baked for travellers embarking on a longish journey, and from the recipes I have seen I suspect the emphasis was more on sustenance than on flavour. My mother's Johnny Cake was totally different. It was so tasty I suspect any traveller would have eaten the whole cake before he had gone more than a mile or two.

Apricot Cakes

3 oz (75 gm) S.R. flour
2 oz (50 gm) butter
2 oz (50 gm) castor sugar
1 egg
Vanilla essence
1 teaspn plain flour

1 teaspn castor sugar
3 teaspns apricot jam
2 tablespns hot water
½ oz (15 gm) finely chopped
    flaked almonds

Sieve the flour. Beat the butter and 2 oz (50 gm) castor sugar to a cream and add the beaten egg and vanilla essence. Stir in the flour. Butter some patty pans. Mix the teaspoon of plain flour with the teaspoon of castor sugar and dust the patty pans with this mixture. Fill the patty pans three parts full with the cake mixture and bake in a moderate oven for about twenty-five minutes. Meanwhile mix the jam with the hot water, rub through a sieve. When the cakes are done turn them out upside down, cover them with the jam and sprinkle with the flaked almonds.

Banana Bunloaf

6 oz (175 gm) plain flour
2 teaspns baking powder
¼ teaspn bicarbonate soda
    (baking soda)
½ teaspn salt

3 oz (75 gm) cooking fat
6 oz (175 gm) sugar
2 eggs
6 oz (175 gm) mashed banana

Sieve together the flour, baking powder, bicarbonate of soda and salt.

Cream the fat and gradually beat in the sugar. Add the eggs, well beaten and then add dry ingredients alternately with the mashed banana. Beat until well combined. Pour into a greased and lined tin nine by five inches (23 cm × 12 cm) and stand aside for twenty minutes. Bake for approximately one hour in a moderate oven until golden brown. When cold slice thinly and spread with butter.

Barm Brack

1 oz (25 gm) yeast
3 oz (75 gm) castor sugar
Milk to mix
1 lb (450 gm) flour

2 oz (50 gm) butter
6 oz (175 gm) sultanas
Pinch mixed spice
1 egg

Cream the yeast with a little of the sugar. Add two table-spoons of the warmed milk and sprinkle one tablespoon of the flour over it. Leave to froth in a warm place. Rub the butter into the remaining flour, add the sugar, sultanas, spice and salt and mix well together. Add the frothed yeast and the beaten egg and mix together, adding more warm milk if necessary. The dough should not be too stiff neither should it be too soft to handle. Knead lightly for about five minutes and put back into the warm basin, cover and stand in a warm place until it has risen to twice its size. Turn out on to a floured board. Shape into three rounds and put on a greased warm baking sheet. Leave to rise again in a warm place for twenty to thirty minutes. Brush the tops gently with milk and bake in a moderately hot oven for forty-five minutes.

If you like a sticky top mix two teaspoons of sugar with warm water and about five minutes before cooking time is up brush the tops of the bracks with this. Return to the oven to finish cooking.

Broken Biscuit Slices

1 oz (25 gm) butter
1 tablespn golden syrup
1 tablespn cocoa

¼ lb (100 gm) biscuit crumbs
(*not* cream crackers or similar)
2 oz (50 gm) dark cooking
chocolate

Melt the butter and syrup in a pan but do not allow it to become too hot. Remove from the heat. Stir in the cocoa and beat in the biscuit crumbs. Press the mixture into a shallow greased tin and bake in a slow to moderate oven for about half an hour. Leave in tin until cold. Melt cooking chocolate in basin over pan of hot water, spread on cake. Cut into squares or fingers.

Bruach Winter Cake
(no milk or eggs)

4 oz (100 gm) seeded raisins or
  sultanas
2 oz (50 gm) dates
2 oz (50 gm) currants
1 oz (25 gm) candied peel
4 oz (100 gm) dripping
4 oz (100 gm) brown sugar

¼ pint (150 ml) water
1 teaspn mixed spice
½ lb (225 gm) S.R. flour
Pinch salt
1 teaspn bicarb or soda dissolved
  in little milk or water

Put the fruit, fat, sugar, water and spice into a pan. Bring to simmering point and keep simmering for ten minutes. Set aside to cool. Sieve together the flour and salt, stir in the fruit and then quickly stir in the bicarbonate of soda and milk or water. Turn into a greased bread tin and bake in a moderate oven for about one hour.

Caramel Sponge Sandwich

For the caramel:
20 small cubes of sugar
¼ pint (150 ml) hot milk

6 oz (175 gm) flour

Pinch salt
1 level teaspn baking powder
4 oz (100 gm) butter
4 oz (100 gm) castor sugar
2 eggs

Make the caramel by melting the sugar lumps in a saucepan and heating until a light coffee colour. Cool a little, add the hot milk and stir until the caramel has dissolved in it. Leave until lukewarm.

Sieve the flour, salt and baking powder together. Cream the butter and sugar and beat in the yolks of the eggs. Beat in the lukewarm caramel. Stir in the dry ingredients and mix well, adding more milk if required. The mixture should be of a soft dropping consistency. Whip the egg whites stiffly and fold in. Put into greased sandwich tin, allowing plenty of room to rise and bake in a moderately hot oven for about three-quarters of an hour or until the cake is firm to the touch. Cool on a wire tray, split and spread with apricot and walnut filling.

Apricot and walnut filling: Rub four tablespoons apricot

jam through a sieve and mix it with a teaspoonful of lemon juice. Stir in about two ounces chopped walnuts.

Ceilidh Shortbread

4 oz (100 gm) butter
2 oz (50 gm) castor sugar
½ teaspn ratafia essence
½ lb (225 gm) S.R. flour

1 oz (25 gm) flaked almonds
2 egg yolks
Castor sugar for dredging

Cream the butter and sugar and beat in the ratafia essence. Sift in the flour. Add the almonds and beaten egg yolks. Knead lightly; press into a greased sandwich tin. Prick with a fork and bake in a moderate oven for about forty minutes until pale brown. Dredge with castor sugar and cut into triangles.

Chocolate Eclairs

2 oz (50 gm) butter
¼ pint (150 ml) boiling water
4 oz (100 gm) flour
3 small eggs

¼ teaspn baking powder
Whipped cream
Chocolate icing

Put the butter in a saucepan, add the boiling water and stir over gentle heat until the butter has melted. Stir in the flour, beating hard until the mixture is thick and smooth and leaves the side of the pan. Remove from the heat and allow to cool for a few minutes. Add the unbeaten eggs one at a time, beating thoroughly until the mixture is smooth before adding the next one. The paste should be of a soft consistency and suitable for piping. Quickly beat in the baking powder and put the paste into a forcing bag with a half-inch (1 cm) plain round tube and force it into strips about three to four inches long on to a greased baking tray. Bake in a moderately hot oven for twenty-five to thirty minutes or until they are pale golden brown and crisp. When cold make a slit in the side and insert whipped cream. Coat tops with chocolate icing.

Most recipe books do not recommend baking powder

when making the pastry for éclairs but I find mine are successful only when I do include some form of raising.

I was making cinnamon cookies one day and if there is one spice which makes a kitchen smell more attractive than scorching cinnamon I have yet to discover it.

'My, My!' exclaimed my erstwhile landlady, Morag, opening the kitchen door. 'I believe the smell you have in here would fetch a seal in from the skerries, it's that good.' She sat down and bit into a warm cookie. 'I could eat these supposin' I had no throat to swallow them,' she declared enthusiastically but when I told her to take some home for herself she declined. 'Indeed I'll not do that but what I will do is take some for young Chaunette that's been so poorly for the last week or two. The doctor says she should be takin' food now but the poor lassie has no fancy for it an' her own mother's not the one for tempting her to eat.'

Young Chaunette was the daughter of a somewhat feckless family who had taken over a derelict but-and-ben not far from Bruach and, having made it habitable according to their standards, appeared to be settling themselves in. They had hens and a cow and they cut rough hay from the moor around them and already they had staked a claim to a peat hag. The Bruachites referred to them as 'cottars' which meant they had no title to their land and as such they were despised though not rejected by the village.

Some days later Morag came again. 'Those cookies as you called them,' she began, 'I took them to Chaunette an' when she'd tasted one she ate three, one after the other. Aye, her that has no taken a bite of food these four days past.' She looked at me to see if I was suitably impressed. 'Aye, an' the doctor's that pleased with her he's after sayin' he's a mind to ask you to sell him some cookies to give the rest of his patients. He's sayin' they're better for them than his medicine,' she added flatteringly.

I regarded the cookies as no more than stand-bys to replenish the biscuit tin but undoubtedly they were popular with my neighbours. Here is the recipe.

Cinnamon Cookies

4 oz (100 gm) S.R. flour	2 oz (50 gm) castor sugar
Pinch salt	1 teaspn golden syrup
½ teaspn cinnamon	1 egg
2 oz (50 gm) butter	½ oz (15 gm) flaked almonds

Sieve together the flour, salt and cinnamon. Beat the butter and sugar to a cream and stir in the syrup. Beat the egg and add the flour and egg alternately to the butter and sugar mixture. Mix well. Pinch off small pieces of the dough and roll into balls about the size of a walnut. Press them flat, sprinkle with flaked almonds and place on a greased baking sheet. Bake for twenty to twenty-five minutes in a moderate oven until nicely golden brown.

Cream Horns

8 oz (225 gm) flour	Water to mix
Pinch salt	Jam
6 oz (175 gm) butter	Whipped cream or butter cream
1 teaspn lemon juice	

Sieve together the flour and the salt. Cut the butter into small pieces and drop into the flour. Add the lemon juice and just sufficient water to make a stiff dough. Turn out on to a floured board and roll into an oblong. Fold in three by bringing the top one-third down over the centre and folding the bottom one up over it. Give the pastry a half turn so that the folds are to the sides and put into a refrigerator for about ten minutes. Repeat this rolling and folding three times, refrigerating each time to keep the pastry cool.

Roll out the pastry into a twelve-inch oblong and cut into strips lengthwise and about an inch wide. Moisten one end of the strip and press it gently on to the pointed end of a cream horn tin and wind upwards, overlapping the pastry slightly. Place on a baking tray and bake in a hot oven until crisp and slightly golden, about ten to fifteen minutes. Slip off the tins and cool on a wire tray. When cold put a spoonful of red jam into each horn and fill with whipped cream or with soft butter cream. Dredge with sieved icing sugar.

My cream horn tins were home-made. Just rough squares of metal cut from old tins and then twisted into cones as when making paper bags.

Curly Cookies

2 oz (50 gm) butter	½ teaspn bicarb. soda
4 oz (100 gm) castor sugar	flour
Pinch salt	Castor sugar for dredging
2 large eggs	Fat for frying
2 level teaspns cinnamon	

Beat the butter and sugar to a cream. Add the well beaten eggs, cinnamon and bicarb. of soda dissolved in a tablespoon of warm water. Beat all together for a minute or two and then stir in as much flour as will make a soft dough. Roll out to about half an inch (1 cm) thick and cut into strips about three inches (8 cm) long and one inch (2 cm) wide. Twist each strip, pinching the ends and drop into hot fat. Lift out and drain on crumpled kitchen paper when they are golden brown (about ten minutes). Sprinkle with castor sugar. Serve hot.

You can use sour cream instead of butter and if you mix the bicarbonate of soda with brandy instead of water the cookies are even nicer.

Any cookies left over can be heated up and served with a jam sauce.

Date and Mincemeat Slice

Pastry:	Water to mix
12 oz (350 gm) flour	
6 oz (175 gm) butter	*Filling:*
Pinch salt	1 teaspn castor sugar
2 oz (50 gm) castor sugar	3 oz (75 gm) chopped dates
1 egg	3 tablespn mincemeat

Sieve the flour and salt together. Rub in the butter and add the sugar. Mix in the beaten egg and sufficient water to make a fairly stiff dough. Divide into two pieces and roll each piece into an oblong to fit a Swiss-roll tin. Line the Swiss-roll tin

with one layer of the pastry, spread it with mincemeat, top
with dates and sprinkle the castor sugar over all. Cover with
the second layer of paste, moistening the edges and pinching
together firmly. Bake in a moderately hot oven until the
pastry is a nice golden brown – about thirty minutes. Leave
in the tin to cool and dredge the top with castor sugar. Cut
into oblong slices.

Ginger Cookies

½ lb (225 gm) flour	¼ lb (100 gm) sugar
½ teaspn baking powder	½ teaspn lemon juice
¼ lb (100 gm) treacle	¼ oz (8 gm) ground ginger
¼ lb (100 gm) butter	Flaked almonds

Sieve the flour with the baking powder. Melt together the
butter and treacle and stir in the sugar, lemon juice and
ginger. Mix with the flour. Make into small balls and put on
a greased baking sheet. Sprinkle a few flaked almonds over
each biscuit and bake in a hot oven for about ten minutes.

Granny's Bunloaf

This bunloaf keeps for weeks in a tin.

1 lb (450 gm) butter	1 teaspn bicarbonate of soda
2 lb (900 gm) flour	1 lb (450 gm) brown sugar
1 lb (450 gm) mixed fruit	3 eggs
2 teaspns mixed spice	1 pint (600 ml) milk
½ teaspn allspice	1 tablespn treacle

Sieve the flour and rub in the butter. Mix the fruit, spices,
soda and sugar together. Stir into the flour. Beat the eggs
and add with the treacle and mix in sufficient milk to make
the mixture nicely moist. It should not be too soft. Put into
two well-greased and lined bread tins and bake in a slow to
moderate oven for one and a half hours or until the loaves
are firm.

Hazelnut Bunloaf

As soon as the autumn came round the children of Bruach used to rush off on Saturday mornings for 'nutting expeditions'. The 'wood' they made for was about three miles from the village and was only a small cove fringed by hazel trees but in all my years in Bruach I cannot recall an autumn when the trees were not laden with nuts. The children gathered the nuts and ate them while the shells were still green and soft and by the time the nuts were ripe the children had tired of them which left the field, or rather the wood, clear for me. I used to make this delicious hazelnut bunloaf:

8 oz (225 gm) flour	1 egg
1 teaspn baking powder	1 tablespn syrup
Pinch salt	Pinch mixed spice
3 oz (75 gm) butter or margarine	6 oz (175 gm) hazelnuts
2 oz (50 gm) sugar	Milk to mix

Blanch and mince or chop the hazelnuts; if they are fresh picked (when they contain a good deal of oil) cut down the butter or margarine by half. Sieve the flour, baking powder, salt and spice together into a basin. Stir in the sugar and the hazelnuts. Make a well in the centre and drop in a lightly beaten egg. Warm the syrup slightly and pour in on top of the egg. Mix altogether with sufficient milk to make the mixture of a soft dropping consistency. Pour into a lightly greased bread tin and bake in a moderate oven for about forty minutes until the cake is firm and well risen. When cool cut into slices and spread with butter.

Iced Fruit Slices

8 oz (225 gm) flour	2 oz (50 gm) sugar
Pinch salt	2 oz (50 gm) sultanas
1 teaspn baking powder	1 egg
Pinch mixed spice	Milk to mix
2 oz (50 gm) butter	Glacé icing

Sieve together the flour, salt, spice and baking powder. Rub in the butter. Add the sugar and fruit. Beat in the egg with sufficient milk to make a very soft dough. Spread the mixture in a Swiss-roll tin, levelling the top with a knife and bake in a hot oven for fifteen to twenty minutes. Leave in tin to cool. When cold, ice with glacé icing and cut into fingers.

Make the glacé icing by mixing sieved icing sugar with warm water and add a drop of lemon juice.

Irish Brack

1 breakfast cup (100 ml) cold tea	8 oz (225 gm) flour (self-raising)
1 lb (450 gm) mixed fruit	2 well-beaten eggs
(currants, raisins, sultanas)	1 teaspn mixed spice
8 oz (225 gm) brown sugar	

Soak the mixed fruit and brown sugar overnight in the tea.

Next morning stir the flour into the fruit and add the well-beaten eggs. Mix well and put into a well-greased and lined loaf tin. Bake for two hours on the middle shelf of a moderate oven. Take out and leave until cool before turning out. It is best left for twenty-four hours before cutting. Slice thinly and spread with butter.

Marmalade Teabread

4 tablespns marmalade	8 oz (225 gm) plain flour
4 tablespns water	1 level teaspn bicarbonate of
3 oz (75 gm) lard	soda
½ teaspn mixed spice	2 eggs
½ teaspn salt	

Put the marmalade, water, lard, spice and salt into a pan over low heat until the fat is melted. Leave until cold. Sieve together the flour and bicarbonate of soda into a basin. Make a well in the centre and stir in the marmalade mixture along with the lightly beaten eggs. Mix well then pour into a greased loaf tin. Bake in the centre of a moderate oven for about one hour until firm and well risen.

This recipe makes a semi-sweet teabread.

Apricot jam can be used instead of marmalade.

Morag's Teabread

'Will you bake me a loaf of your good teabread?' Morag used to ask me when she was expecting a visitor. 'Teabread' to Morag was 'Bunloaf' to me. This is one she particularly liked.

2 oz (50 gm) fresh bran	1 cup (100 ml) water
8 oz (225 gm) brown sugar	1 cup (100 ml) milk
6 oz (175 gm) mixed fruit	1 egg
4 oz (100 gm) white flour	1 level teaspn mixed spice
4 oz (100 gm) wholewheat or wheatmeal flour	1 level teaspn baking soda
1½ oz (40 gm) butter	Pinch salt

Soak the bran, sugar and fruit in the water for one hour. Sieve the flour, salt, baking soda and spice together. Rub in the butter. Add the soaked fruit and bran and stir. Beat the egg and milk together and stir into the mixture which should now be of a fairly sloppy consistency. Put into a greased loaf tin and bake in a moderate oven for about forty-five minutes until firm. To serve slice and spread with butter.

Mother's Johnny Cake

½ lb (225 gm) Biscuit pastry (recipe page 204)	½ teaspn allspice
4 oz (100 gm) currants	½ oz (15 gm) butter
2 oz (50 gm) moist brown sugar	1 teaspn milk
	1 teaspn castor sugar

Roll out the pastry to about quarter-inch (½ cm) thick and in a rough circle. Spread the currants over the centre of the round keeping them away from the edges. Sprinkle on the sugar and spice. Shave the butter into small pieces and dot over the fruit. Moisten the edges of the pastry and gather together. Roll gently with a rolling pin. Turn over and roll again until the currants show through the pastry. Brush over with milk and bake on a greased baking sheet in a moderately hot oven until golden brown. Sprinkle with castor sugar while still hot.

Old-fashioned Gingerbread

6 oz (175) gm butter
5 oz (125 gm) sugar
1 cup black treacle
½ cup golden syrup
1 teaspn ground ginger
1 teaspn cinnamon

½ teaspn ground cloves (optional)
2 eggs
1 teaspn bicarbonate soda
¾ lb (350 gm) flour
1 cupful (100 ml) sour milk
Hot water

Put the butter, sugar, treacle, syrup, cinnamon, ginger and cloves if used into a pan and heat gently until the butter is melted, stirring to prevent sticking. While the mixture is still warm add the sour milk. Pour into a baking bowl. Add the beaten eggs. Dissolve the bicarbonate of soda in half a cup of hot water and add. Quickly stir in the flour and mix all well together. Turn into a greased tin and bake in a slow to moderate oven for about one hour until nicely firm and brown. This gingerbread keeps well.

Orange Buns

½ lb (225 gm) flour
Pinch salt
3 teaspns baking powder
2 oz (50 gm) butter or lard

2 oz (50 gm) sugar
1 orange
Milk to mix
Sugar cubes

Sieve the flour, salt and baking powder into a bowl and rub in the butter or lard. Add the sugar and the grated rind of the orange and mix to a semi-stiff dough with the milk. Roll into balls then flatten. Put on a greased baking tray. Dip each sugar cube into the juice of the orange and put three on the top of each bun. Bake in a hot oven for ten minutes.

Quick Coconut Pyramids

½ lb (225 gm) desiccated coconut
¼ lb (100 gm) castor sugar

1 egg

Mix together the coconut and sugar. Stir in the egg and press the mixture together with the hands. Dip an eggcup in water, shake, and fill with the mixture. Turn out on to rice paper and bake in a moderately hot oven for ten to twelve minutes or until just beginning to turn golden. It is a good idea to make half the mixture into white pyramids and then to stir a drop or two of pink colouring into the remainder.

Sorrel Slices

½ lb (225 gm) plain flour	Water to mix
Pinch salt	1 tablespn golden syrup
¼ lb (100 gm) butter	1 cupful sorrel leaves
2 oz (50 gm) castor sugar	Pinch mixed spice
1 egg	Icing sugar

Sieve the flour and salt together, rub in the butter, add the sugar and egg and mix to a fairly stiff dough with water. Roll out to a quarter of an inch thick and cut into two equal size oblongs. Line a Swiss-roll tin with one of the pieces. Melt the syrup slightly. Chop the sorrel leaves and add and mix in the spice. Spread this mixture on the pastry in the tin. Lay the remaining pastry on top; moisten the edges and pinch firmly together. Bake in a moderately hot oven for about twenty to twenty-five minutes until pale golden brown. Leave in the tin to cool, dust with icing sugar and cut into slices.

Sheehan Cakes

6 oz (175 gm) butter	2 tablespns milk (approx.)
6 oz (175 gm) castor sugar	Sieved raspberry jam for
3 eggs	decoration
6 oz (175 gm) S.R. flour	

Cream the butter and sugar and add the beaten eggs gradually, beating them in well. Fold in the flour. Add sufficient milk to bring the mixture to a soft consistency Put into a Swiss-roll tin, lightly greased and dusted with flour, and bake in a moderate oven for twenty to twenty five minutes or until the cake is firm to the touch. Cool on a wire tray.

Butter cream:	1 egg yolk
2 oz (50 gm) gran sugar	3 oz (75 gm) butter
3 tablespns water	½ teaspn vanilla essence

Put the water and sugar in a pan over gentle heat until the sugar is dissolved then boil rapidly until it is of a syrupy consistency. Pour the syrup on to the lightly beaten egg yolk and beat until pale and spongy. Pour on to the butter gradually and beat well until smooth. Add vanilla essence. Beat again.

Icing:　　　　　　　　　　　　　3–4 tablespns water
8 oz (225 gm) icing sugar　　　　Red colouring

Mix icing sugar and water together until of a pouring consistency.

Using a $1\frac{1}{2}$ in. (3 cm) plain cutter cut cake into rounds. Spread top of each round first with sieved jam and then lavishly with butter cream which should be shaped into a pyramid. Place the cakes in a refrigerator (or cool place) until the butter cream is firm – about one hour.

Pour half the icing over half the cakes. Colour the remainder of the icing and pour over the rest of the cakes.

Strawberry Cake

2 eggs and their weight in butter,　　Milk to mix
　sugar and flour　　　　　　　　　Strawberry jam
Pinch salt　　　　　　　　　　　　$\frac{1}{4}$ pint (150 ml) double cream
1 teaspn baking powder　　　　　　Icing sugar

Sieve the flour, baking powder and salt together. Beat the butter and sugar to a cream. Add the well-beaten eggs and beat again. Lightly fold in the flour alternately with the milk until the mixture is of a soft dropping consistency. Pour the mixture into two greased and floured eight-inch (20 cm) sandwich tins and bake in a moderate oven for twenty-five to thirty minutes. Cool on a wire tray.

Whip the cream lightly and spread half of it on one of the sponge rounds. Using a cutter an inch (2 cm) in diameter cut nine rounds from the other sponge – eight from round the edge and one from the centre. Place the sponge from which the pieces have been cut on top of the other one and into each hole place a teaspoon of strawberry jam. Divide the remaining cream among the holes and rest the cut rounds gently on top so that they are raised from the cake. Dredge the cake lightly with icing sugar.

Strupak Biscuits

8 oz (225 gm) S.R. flour	1 egg
Pinch salt	Glacé icing
½ teaspn mixed spice	Raspberry jam or jelly
4 oz (100 gm) butter	Glacé cherries
4 oz (100 gm) castor sugar	

Sieve the flour, salt and spice together. Beat the butter and sugar to a cream. Stir in the flour and add enough beaten egg to make a stiff paste. Roll out to about a quarter of an inch (½ cm) thick, cut into rounds and bake for about thirty minutes in a slow oven. Cool on a wire tray.

When cold spread half the biscuits with jam and top with the remainder of the biscuits. Cover the tops with glacé icing and decorate each with a small piece of glacé cherry.

Teacakes

½ lb (225 gm) flour	2 tablespn warm water
¼ teaspn salt	1 egg
1 oz (25 gm) butter or lard	2 oz (50 gm) sultanas
2 teaspn sugar	Warm milk to mix
½ oz (15 gm) yeast	

Sieve the flour and salt into a basin. Rub in the butter or lard and add half the sugar and the sultanas. Make a well in the centre. Cream the yeast with the warm water. Add the beaten egg and pour into the flour. Mix to a soft dough with milk. Knead and put to rise in a warm place free from draughts until it doubles its size. Divide into two. Knead again and put into greased and floured cake tins. Leave to prove in a warm place for fifteen to twenty minutes. Bake in a hot oven for fifteen to twenty minutes. Brush over with a little milk in which the remaining teaspoon of sugar has been dissolved a few minutes before removing from the oven.

I cannot resist giving the following recipe simply because when it was first given to me by an elderly spinster I found the description so intriguing.

Undressed Bride's Cake

1 lb (450 gm) flour	1 tablespn treacle
1 teaspn baking powder	3 eggs
½ lb (225 gm) butter	½ teacupful (50 ml) milk
½ lb (225 gm) sugar	½ lb (225 gm) currants
1 tablespn golden syrup	

Sieve together the flour and baking powder.

Cream the butter and sugar, add the syrup and treacle and beat in the eggs. Add the flour and milk and lastly the fruit. Mix well together and turn into a greased cake tin. Bake for two to two and a half hours in a very moderate oven.

Waffles

Once at an auction sale I succumbed to the temptation to buy myself what was referred to by the auctioneer as an 'oddments chest'. It cost me ten shillings and, as I found when I got it home and started to unpack it I had bought myself a bargain parcel indeed. Among the 'oddments' was an electric waffle maker, shinily new and in perfect working order. Now fifteen years later it is still in perfect working order and is a great success, particularly when children come to tea because I can make the waffles on the table and let the children fill their own. It is astonishing how even the most pernickety children develop an impatience for food when they see the light, crisp, golden-brown waffles being lifted from the iron and slid on to their plates all ready to have the indentations filled with golden syrup or honey. The waffles can, of course, be filled with a savoury mixture if preferred. Waffle batter should not be allowed to stand before cooking.

Waffles

6 oz (175 gm) flour	½ pint (300 ml) milk
Pinch salt	2 oz (50 gm) melted butter or
1½ teaspns baking powder	cooking oil
1 tablespn castor sugar	Vanilla essence
2 eggs, separated	Oil for cooking

Sift the flour, baking powder and salt together into a basin. Stir in the sugar and make a well in the centre. Add the egg yolks and mix these in. Add the milk and melted butter or oil alternately. Stir in a few drops of vanilla essence. Whip up the whites of the eggs very stiffly and fold lightly into the batter which should now be of the consistency of thick cream. Brush the waffle iron with oil and heat it. Pour in just enough batter to coat the surface being careful not to overfill so that the waffles will be prevented from rising. Cook until golden brown which should take approximately three or four minutes.

Walnut Biscuits

4 oz (100 gm) S.R. flour	4 oz (100 gm) sugar
1 teaspn cornflour	2 oz (50 gm) walnuts
Pinch salt	1 egg yolk
4 oz (100 gm) butter	Few drops vanilla essence

Sieve the flour and cornflour and salt together. Cream the butter and sugar. Beat in the flour and cornflour gradually. Stir in the chopped walnuts. Add vanilla essence. Mix with enough egg yolk to make fairly stiff paste. Roll into balls, flatten and prick with a fork. Bake for fifteen to twenty minutes in a moderate oven. Cool on a wire tray.

Scones

It seems a pity that the habit of taking afternoon tea seems now to have gone out of fashion because in my childhood afternoon tea-time coincided with coming home from school time and as soon as they came in through the door most children could be certain of being given something to stave off the pangs of hunger until their proper tea-time. Usually it was a variety of scone for in those days mothers vied with one another over their scone baking and the better scone baker a woman was the more friends her children had even if all they got sometimes was a small piece grudgingly broken off a corner of the scone.

I didn't much care for our local policeman's daughter but I allowed her to be my friend on Tuesdays and Friday's because those were her mother's baking days and her mother made the most wonderful scones I have ever tasted. Being a Scot the policeman's wife could be counted on for her generosity and she used to come out to where we were playing (I saw to it that it was never far from the kitchen) and give us each a whole scone, still warm from the oven, all spicy smelling and dripping with butter. How my mouth watered for those scones!

Perhaps childhood appetite enhanced their flavour for though I have sought the recipe for years I have never managed to produce anything that quite came up to their remembered perfection. The recipe on page 181 for fruit scones is the nearest I have been able to achieve.

Barley-meal Scones

½ lb (225 gm) barley meal	Hot milk to mix
1 teaspn salt	

Sieve together the salt and barley meal and mix with hot

milk until it becomes a thick paste. Roll out to one quarter of an inch ($\frac{1}{2}$ cm) thick, cut into triangles and cook on a hot girdle which has been well greased turning when one side is nicely brown.

Alternatively cook in a hot oven for ten to fifteen minutes. Barley meal scones should be eaten hot with butter or fried with bacon.

Scone baking in Bruach was always done with plain flour and with bicarbonate of soda and cream of tartar as raising agents. They never used self-raising flour possibly because flour had to be stored for considerable periods of time and self-raising flour did not keep as well as plain flour. Nor did I ever see them use baking powder though I daresay it might serve just as well.

Another point about Bruach cooking was that they liked everything to be well salted. In the following recipe I have given half a teaspoonful of salt as the required quantity but in fact it was a full teaspoon my neighbours always used. You should adjust the quantity according to your taste.

Bruach Girdle Scones

$\frac{1}{2}$ lb (225 gm) flour	$\frac{1}{2}$ teaspn salt
1 teaspn bicarbonate of soda	Milk to mix
1 teaspn cream of tartar	

Sieve the flour, salt, bicarbonate of soda and cream of tartar together in a bowl. Make a well in the centre and using a knife to mix add milk until you have a dough that is soft yet workable. The test is to pinch a little of the dough between the thumb and forefinger and pull gently: the pinch of dough should not come away cleanly but should stretch rather like tired elastic. Working quickly all the time turn the dough on to a well-floured board and press out gently with the hand into a round about half an inch (1 cm) thick, remembering always to press from the outside of the round towards the centre. Cut into quarters and place on a hot greased girdle. Alternatively you can leave the round whole but I find the dough tends to be rather unmanageable this way. Turn the scones when one side is golden brown and cook the other side. To test when sufficiently cooked gently break open the edge of a scone. If it looks at all sticky cook it a little longer.

Bruach Oatcakes

½ lb (225 gm) medium oatmeal	1 tablespn melted lard or butter
½ teaspn salt	Cold water to mix
½ teaspn bicarbonate of soda	

Mix the oatmeal, salt and bicarbonate of soda together. Work in the melted lard or butter with the hands and add the cold water gradually until it is possible to squeeze the oatmeal into a ball without the outside of the ball looking at all wet. It is fatal to add too much water to oatcakes. Turn on to a well-oatmealed board; with the hands press into a round about a quarter of an inch (½ cm) thick. Cut into triangles and cook on a hot greased girdle for about five minutes each side. Finish by drying off in front of an open fire for about fifteen to twenty minutes or until they are crisp. Do not put them too close to the fire.

I wish I could say there was a substitute for an open fire for finishing off the oatcakes but I fear I have not found one.

Bruach Potato Scones

½ lb (225 gm) cooked and mashed potatoes	Pinch salt
1 oz (25 gm) melted butter	½ teaspn bicarbonate of soda
4 oz (50 gm) flour	½ teaspn cream of tartar

Mix the melted butter with the hot mashed potato and allow to cool. Sieve the flour, salt, bicarbonate of soda and cream of tartar together and work into the cooked potato. Roll out very thinly on a floured board: cut into oblongs and cook on a moderately hot girdle until pale brown on both sides. As they come off the girdle place them on a cloth and cover with another cloth. While they are still hot spread them with butter, roll up and serve.

Bruach Scads

½ pint (300 ml) water
1 teaspn salt

Flour
Oatmeal

Boil the water and salt in a pan. Remove from the heat and beat in enough flour to make a thick paste. Continue to beat until the mixture leaves the sides of the pan. Tip out on to a floured board and leave to cool.

When cold strew the board well with oatmeal and roll out the dough very thinly. Turn over so that both sides are coated with the oatmeal: cut into triangles and cook on a moderately hot girdle until they just begin to brown. Turn and cook the other side. Lift on to a hot plate; spread with butter; roll up and serve hot.

Cheese Scones

½ lb (225 gm) flour
1 teaspn baking powder
Pinch salt
Pinch of pepper
Pinch of dry mustard

2 oz (50 gm) of butter or fat
2 oz (50 gm) grated cheese
1 egg
Milk to mix

Sieve the flour, baking powder, salt, pepper and mustard together. Rub in the fat. Add the grated cheese and stir in the lightly beaten egg with enough milk to make a soft light dough. Turn the dough out on to a floured board and press lightly into a round about three-quarters of an inch (1½ cm) thick. Cut into triangles, brush with milk and bake in a hot oven for about twenty minutes until golden brown.

Drop Scones
(or Scotch Pancakes)

½ lb (225 gm) flour
1 teaspn bicarbonate of soda and
  1 teaspn cream of tartar,
  or 2 teaspns baking powder
Pinch of salt

Tablespn castor sugar (omit if the
  pancakes are to be eaten with
  savoury dishes)
1 large egg or two small eggs
Milk to mix

Sieve the flour, salt, bicarbonate of soda and cream of tartar together in a basin. Stir in the sugar. Make a well in the centre and drop in the egg, unbeaten. With a metal spoon stir the egg into the flour while adding the milk. Work quickly. The mixture should be the consistency of medium-thick cream unless a thinner scone is preferred when more milk should be added.

Have ready a hot greased girdle and drop spoonfuls of the batter on to it. When bubbles begin to burst on the surface of the batter the scones are ready to be turned. Use a palette knife for turning and brown the scones on both sides. Wrap in a clean linen cloth to cool.

Flapjack

¼ lb (100 gm) flour	Pinch pepper
Pinch salt	Water to mix

Sieve the flour and salt and pepper into a basin and mix to a thick creamy consistency with cold water. Have ready a moderately hot well-greased frying pan (preferably using bacon fat for greasing) and fry on both sides until pale golden brown. Serve hot with bacon.

My first winter in my own cottage in Bruach was an austere one, due to my having underestimated the stores I needed to lay in. I was reduced to eating flapjack for days at a time.

Fruit Scones

½ lb (225 gm) flour	¼ teaspn cinnamon
1 teaspn baking powder	1 teaspn custard powder
Pinch salt	¼ pint (150 ml) sour cream or
1 oz (25 gm) butter	milk
1 egg	(If using milk use extra ounce
1 oz (25 gm) sugar	(25 gm) of butter)
2 oz (50 gm) sultanas	

Sieve the flour, salt, cinnamon, baking powder and custard powder together into a basin and rub in the butter and stir in the sugar and sultanas. Beat the egg with the cream. Pour into the flour and mix from the centre outwards, drawing the flour in gradually. Work quickly and lightly. The dough should be soft yet firm enough to handle. Turn on to a floured board and press gently into a round about half an inch (10 cm) thick using the palm of the hand. Cut into triangles or rounds. If baking in the oven the scones should be brushed with milk and placed on a greased baking tray in a hot oven. If cooking on a girdle omit the brushing with milk.

In the oven the scones should take about ten to fifteen minutes. On the girdle (which should be greased and dusted with flour) cook for about six minutes each side.

The fruit may be omitted if a plain scone is preferred.

Oatmeal Bannocks

4 oz (100 gm) flour
1 teaspn bicarbonate of soda
1 teaspn cream of tartar
Pinch salt
Pinch cinnamon

4 oz (100 gm) medium oatmeal
1 tablespn golden syrup
2 eggs
Milk to mix

Sieve together the flour, bicarbonate of soda, cream of tartar, salt and cinnamon into a bowl. Mix in the oatmeal. Make a well in the centre and drop in one egg then the syrup and then the other egg. With a metal spoon mix the eggs and syrup into the flour and oatmeal, adding the milk until the mixture is the consistency of fairly thick cream. The batter for bannocks is usually rather thinner than that for drop scones. Cook on a hot greased girdle, as for drop scones. Wrap in a clean cloth and cool on a wire tray.

Potato Scones – Thick

4 oz (100 gm) S.R. flour
½ teaspn salt
¼ lb (225 gm) cooked mashed
  potatoes

½ oz (25 gm) melted butter
Milk to mix, approx. ¼ pint
  (150 ml)

Sieve the S.R. flour and the salt together. Melt the butter in a pan add the milk and make lukewarm. Mix the butter and milk with the potatoes and work in enough flour to make a nice dough – not too stiff. Roll out on a floured board to half-inch (1 cm) thickness: cut into triangles and bake in a hot oven until golden brown (about twenty minutes). Serve hot with lashings of butter and golden syrup or honey.

Sultana Pancakes

4 oz (100 gm) flour	1 oz (50 gm) sultanas
1 teaspn baking powder	1 egg
Pinch salt	¼ pint (150 ml) milk
1 oz (25 gm) sugar	

Sieve together the flour, baking powder and salt into a basin. Stir in the sugar and add the sultanas. Beat the egg lightly and stir into the mixture with sufficient milk to make a batter the consistency of thick cream. Grease and heat a girdle and drop on spoonfuls of the batter. Turn when the bubbles begin to burst and cook the other side. The girdle should not be too hot and the pancakes should take about two minutes either side to cook. Wrap in a clean cloth and cool on a wire tray. They are best eaten while still warm.

Wholemeal Scones

6 oz (175 gm) wholemeal flour	½ teaspn salt
2 oz (50 gm) white flour	2 oz (50 gm) butter
½ teaspn bicarbonate of soda	1 egg
1 teaspn cream of tartar	Milk to mix

Sieve together the wholemeal, white flour, bicarbonate of soda, cream of tartar and salt. Rub in the butter, add the beaten egg and mix to a soft dough with the milk. Roll out to three-quarters of an inch (1½ cm) thick. Cut into triangles and brush with milk. Bake in a hot oven for about fifteen to twenty minutes.

If a sweet scone is preferred add either one tablespoon of sugar or black treacle before adding the beaten egg.

Sauces

'Oh, how I love the gorgeous smell of that caramel custard you're always making,' announced the Bruach nurse, sniffing her way into my kitchen. 'I wish I had the time to indulge myself with food the way you do,' she added enviously. Since the population of Bruach was little more than a hundred souls most of whom were phenomenally healthy one would never have suspected the nurse could be overworked but overworked she claimed to be and as she rushed from one crofthouse to another, gasping for cups of tea to sustain her, she left us in no doubt of her devotion to duty.

It was hardly flattering that the nurse accused me of making caramel custard so often since it was by no means one of my favourite sweets and the 'gorgeous smell' she claimed to detect so frequently coming from my kitchen was invariably a pan of milk and sugar which had been set on the stove in preparation for making an ordinary 'custard powder sauce' (I prefer it to egg custard) and which, due to my inattention, had boiled over. However, I never enlightened the nurse as to the true source of the smell. She was that sort of woman.

Apple Sauce

---

1 lb (450 gm) cooking apples	1 teaspn lemon juice
1 teaspn sugar	½ oz (15 gm) butter

Peel and chop the apples and put into a saucepan with just enough water to prevent them burning. Cook until the apple is soft enough to be beaten to a pulp. Add the sugar and lemon juice and beat in along with the butter.

Bechamel Sauce

2 oz (50 gm) flour
2 oz (50 gm) butter
1 pint (600 ml) milk
Bouquet garni
Small onion or shallot

1 celery stalk
1 small bayleaf
Pinch mace
Pinch cayenne pepper

Put the milk into a pan and add the vegetables (roughly chopped) and the seasonings. Bring to the boil. Set aside for about ten minutes to infuse. Melt the butter, stir in the flour. Strain the milk and stir into the flour and butter mixture. Stir into the liquid. Bring to the boil and simmer gently for two or three minutes. Test for seasoning.

Caper Sauce

1 oz (25 gm) butter
1¼ oz (35 gm) flour
¼ pint (150 ml) stock in which
  mutton has been boiled

½ pint (150 ml) milk
1 teaspn vinegar
Pepper and salt
1½ tablespns capers

Melt the butter in a pan, stir in the flour and cook for one minute, continuing to stir. Add the stock and the milk gradually. Boil for three minutes. Add the vinegar, pepper, salt and capers which should be roughly chopped. Continue to cook for a further five minutes.

Cockle Sauce

¼ pint (150 ml) milk
1 oz (25 gm) flour
1 pint (450 gm) cockles

2 oz (50 gm) butter
Juice of 1 lemon
Small pinch pepper

Warm the cockles in a pan without water until they open. Take out the cockles and throw away the shells. Rinse well and chop finely. Mix with the lemon juice and pepper. Melt the butter in a saucepan and gradually stir in the flour. Add milk and cook for one minute. Add the cockles and simmer very gently for three minutes. Do not allow the sauce to boil.

Serve with cod or haddock.

188

Hollandaise Sauce

¼ lb (100 gm) butter cut into
   small pieces
2 egg yolks

Salt and pepper
Lemon juice

Put half the butter in a basin over hot water until melted. Add well-beaten egg yolks and stir until sauce begins to thicken. Add the rest of the butter piece by piece. The sauce should now be of a creamy consistency. Add the seasoning and a squeeze of lemon juice. Keep hot but ensure the sauce does not boil.

Mock Hollandaise Sauce

1 oz (25 gm) butter
1 oz (25 gm) flour
Pepper and salt

½ pint (300 ml) milk or mixture
   of fish stock and milk
1 egg
1 teaspn lemon juice

Melt the butter, add the flour and cook for three minutes without browning. Remove from the heat and gradually stir in the milk. Return to low heat and stir until it boils. Simmer for two minutes, season, remove from the heat. Beat the egg and add and stir in the lemon juice.

Mushroom Sauce

½ lb (225 gm) mushrooms
½ pint (300 ml) chicken stock
1 oz (25 gm) butter
1 tablespn flour
½ teaspn celery seed

1 strip thin lemon rind
Pinch sweet basil
Salt and pepper
¼ pint (150 ml) milk (or cream if
   available)

Boil stock with the celery seed, lemon rind, basil and salt and pepper for about five minutes. Cool.

   Melt the butter in a pan, stir in the flour and cook for one minute. Add the milk and the chicken stock. Re-boil and add the chopped mushrooms. Simmer for about six minutes. Re-season if necessary before serving.

Onion Sauce

2 large onions, chopped coarsely
2 oz (50 gm) butter
2 oz (50 gm) flour
¼ pint (150 ml) milk
⅛ pint (75 ml) onion water
Salt and pepper

Put the onions into cold water and bring them to the boil. Keep simmering until they are tender, about five minutes. Drain them from the water. Melt the butter in a pan, stir in the flour and cook for one minute but do not allow it to brown. Add the milk, onion water, salt and pepper and the chopped onions. Simmer for about five minutes. Re-season if necessary.

Parsley Sauce

1 oz (25 gm) butter
1 oz (25 gm) flour
Salt and pepper
½ pint (300 ml) milk
1 tablespn chopped parsley

Melt the butter, add the flour and cook for three minutes without browning. Remove from the heat and gradually stir in the milk. Return to the heat, season and stir until boiling. Simmer for two minutes. Add parsley and set aside in a warm place with a lid on the pan for a few minutes.

Pork Special Sauce

1 med. sized apple (cooking)
1 small onion
1 oz (25 gm) pork dripping
1 teacup (100 ml) stock
Pinch salt
¼ teaspn cayenne pepper
½ teaspn dry mustard
1 teaspn sugar
Juice of 1 lemon
1 tablespn brandy

Chop the apple and onion finely and fry them in the dripping until they are tender but not brown. Mash them well together. Add the stock, all the seasoning, sugar and lemon juice. Bring to the boil and simmer for two minutes. Just before serving add the brandy.

Sauce Robert

1 oz (25 gm) butter	½ pint (300 ml) stock (vegetable)
2 med. sized onions	1 meat cube
½ oz (15 gm) flour	¼ teaspn mixed mustard
Salt and pepper	

Melt the butter in a saucepan. Slice the onion and fry in the butter until golden brown. Add the flour and stir while cooking for about two minutes. Add the salt and pepper, the stock and the meat cube and stir in the mustard. Bring the sauce to the boil; simmer for about fifteen minutes.

Shrimp Sauce

2 oz (50 gm) shrimps	Salt and pepper
1 oz (25 gm) butter	Small pinch cayenne pepper
1 tablespn flour	1 teaspn lemon juice
1 cup (100 ml) water	

Melt the butter in a saucepan. Stir in the flour and cook for one minute. Add the water and bring to the boil. Remove from the heat, add lemon juice, cayenne, seasoning and shrimps. Stand over gentle heat for about four minutes but do not allow it to boil. Boiling will toughen the shrimps. Serve with almost any fish dish.

Tomato Sauce

1 oz (25 gm) butter	Seasoning
1 level tablespn flour	1 teaspn lemon juice
1 cupful (100 ml) of tomato juice	1 teaspn sugar

Melt the butter in a saucepan, stir in the flour and cook for one minute. Add tomato juice, salt, pepper, sugar and lemon juice. Heat through.

White Sauce

1 oz (25 gm) butter	Salt and pepper
1 oz (25 gm) flour	¼ pint (150 ml) milk

191

Melt the butter, stir in the flour and cook for a few minutes without browning. Remove from the heat and gradually stir in the milk. Bring to the boil, add the seasoning and continue to simmer for three or four minutes.

Brandy Butter (1)

¼ lb (100 gm) butter
¼ lb (100 gm) soft brown sugar

3 tablespn brandy

Cream the butter until pale and soft. Beat in the sugar gradually and add the brandy a little at a time so that the mixture does not curdle.

Brandy Butter (2)

¼ lb (100 gm) butter
1 oz (25 gm) ground almonds

2 oz (59 gm) caster sugar
3 tablespns brandy

Cream the butter until pale and soft. Beat in the sugar and then the ground almonds. Add the brandy a little at a time.

Brandy Sauce

¼ teaspn cornflour
½ pint (300 ml) milk
1½ oz (40 gm) soft brown sugar

1 egg yolk
3 to 4 tablespns brandy

Blend the cornflour with a little of the milk. Boil the remainder of the milk and pour on to the cornflour. Return to the pan and simmer for five minutes while continuing to stir. Add the sugar and stir until dissolved. Cool slightly. Stir in the egg yolk and then the brandy. Make this sauce immediately before it is required.

Butterscotch Sauce

2 oz (50 gm) gran. sugar
3 tablespns boiling water
½ oz (15 gm) butter

1 teaspn flour
3 tablespns milk

Put the sugar into a thick saucepan and heat gently until it becomes liquid and brown. Shake the pan a little during the cooking but do not stir. Remove from the heat, cool slightly and gradually add the boiling water. Return to the heat and simmer until the caramel is dissolved then set aside. Melt the butter, add the flour and stir in the milk slowly. Add the caramel, bring to the boil, stirring, and cook for about three minutes.

Caramel Brandy Sauce

30 small cubes sugar	Small pinch mace
¼ pint (150 ml) boiling water	2 tablespns brandy
½ oz (15 gm) butter	

Put the sugar lumps into a pan over gentle heat until they become syrupy and golden brown. Add the water slowly and heat until the caramel is dissolved, stirring constantly. Remove from the heat. Add the butter and mace. Cool and add the brandy.

Chocolate Sauce
(with syrup)

2 oz (50 gm) butter	1 heaped tablespn cocoa
2 tablespns golden syrup	

Melt the butter in the saucepan but do not allow it to get hot. Stir in the syrup and cocoa and continue to stir until you have a nice smooth sauce. Do not allow the sauce to become too hot.

Marmalade Orange Sauce

2 good tablespns orange marmalade	1 wineglass water
1 wineglass sherry	6 lumps sugar
	1 tablespn arrowroot or cornflour

Heat together the marmalade, sherry, water and sugar until sugar is dissolved. Stir in the arrowroot or cornflour and simmer for one minute.

Miscellaneous

In the Hebrides burying food has always been a traditional way of preserving it. They buried skarts but usually only for a few days so the skarts could mature without the attentions of flies, cats or dogs but in the old days they buried crocks of butter for months, even years and it is not unusual for casks of whisky to be found under the earthen floors of old croft houses although I suspect visits from the Excise officers may have been responsible for these rather than any intention of preserving the whisky.

During the last war when sugar was scarce I was given this recipe for bottling fruit without sugar – even without water.

Fill the bottles with the sound, dry fruit, cork them and seal over the corks with candlewax. Bury them, cork side down, two feet deep under a tree. It is said that by using this method fruit will stay perfectly good for more than thirty years.

I never did get round to testing this method but preserved any fruit I was able to come by in jams and jellies and wines.

Hawthorn Jelly

Hawthorns make a delicious jelly to eat with lamb or mutton.

2 lb (900 gm) hawthorn berries	Sugar
2 lemons	2 pints (1¼ litres) cold water

Peel the lemons. Put the berries and the lemon rind and juice into a pan with two pints (1¼ litres) cold water. Bring to the boil and simmer for one hour. Strain through a jelly bag and leave overnight to drip. Measure the juice and return to the pan with one pound (450 gm) sugar to every pint (600 ml) of juice. Boil until the jelly sets when tested. Depending on the maturity of the berries a set is achieved fairly quickly.

Rhubarb and Loganberry Jam

1½ lb (½ kg) rhubarb
¼ pint (120 ml) water

1½ lb (½ kg) loganberries
3 lb (1 kg) sugar

Cut up the rhubarb and cook slowly in the water until it is reduced to a thick pulp. Cook the loganberries with the rhubarb for another five minutes then add the sugar. Stir until the sugar has dissolved and then boil rapidly until setting point is reached.

Instead of loganberries you can get almost the same flavour by using a mixture of blackberries (ripe or unripe), raspberries and a dessertspoon of lemon juice along with the rhubarb.

Rowan and Apple Jelly

1 lb (450 gm) rowan berries
1 lb (450 gm) cooking apples

1 lb (450 gm) sugar (approx.)

Put the unpeeled apples and the rowanberries into a pan and boil until soft. Put through a jelly bag. Add one pound (450 gm) of sugar to every pint (600 ml) of juice. Put back into pan and re-boil until it jellies. Eat it by the spoonful as a tonic or serve with cold mutton or venison.

It is said of the rowan, 'Whoever shall eat of the berries of the rowan tree if he has completed a hundred years of his life he will return to the age of thirty.' I have eaten and drunk much of the fruit of the rowan but as I haven't yet reached my century I cannot vouch for the truth of the old saying.

Elderberry Wine

4 lb (1¾ kg) elderberries
1 gallon (5 litres) water
1½ lb (½ kg) sugar
¼ lb (100 gm) raisins

¼in. (2 cm) of a cinnamon stick
1 lemon
1 orange

Strip the berries from the stalks and pour the boiling water over them. Leave to stand for twenty-four hours. Squeeze them well with the hands and strain them through a jelly bag. Put into a large bowl and stir in the sugar, lemon and orange cut into thin slices. Boil the raisins with the cinnamon stick for ten minutes. Cool, strain and add to the rest of the wine. Cover and allow to stand in a warm room for ten days then strain into jars or casks. As the wine ferments keep topped up with more wine until fermentation ceases. Bung tightly and leave for six months before bottling.

Heather Ale

1 gallon (1 kg) can of heather tips	1 lb (450 gm) golden syrup
2 gallons (10 litres) water	1 oz (25 gm) ginger
½ oz (15 gm) hops	1 oz (25 gm) yeast

Gather the heather tips when in full bloom. Put them into a large pan and cover with the water. Boil for one hour. Strain into a clean bowl or jar. In one quart of the liquid boil the hops, golden syrup and ginger for twenty minutes. Strain into the heather water. Leave until lukewarm and add yeast. Cover with a coarse cloth and stand for twenty-four hours. Skim the liquid carefully and pour the clear ale into a tub, leaving the yeasty sediment at the bottom. Bottle and cork tightly. Leave for two or three days before drinking.

Mock Whisky

3 lb (1 kg) brown rice	Juice of 1 lemon
3 lb (1 kg) sugar	8 pints (5 litres) warm water
1 lb (450 gm) raisins	1 oz (25 gm) yeast

Put all the ingredients except the yeast into a large jar or bowl. Mix the yeast with a little warm water until dissolved and add. Stand the jar in a warm place for twelve days (if using a bowl this should be covered with a cloth) stirring occasionally for the first three days. After it has stood twelve days skim the surface and filter the liquid into a clean jar or cask. Store for six months in a cool place and then bottle.

Nettle Beer

1 lb (450 gm) nettles
2 gallons (10 litres) water
½ lb (225 gm) sugar
1 tablespn malt extract

3 or 4 sprigs carragheen moss or
¼ teaspn gelatine
1 oz (25 gm) hops
½ oz (15 gm) dried yeast or 1 oz
(25 gm) fresh yeast

Boil the nettles and hops in the water for about twenty minutes. Remove from the heat and stir in the malt extract and the sugar. Leave until the liquid is lukewarm then add the carragheen or gelatine and the yeast. If fresh yeast is being used cream it first before adding. Leave for twelve to eighteen hours. Siphon off into bottles and cork securely, or skim off the nettle 'cap' and pour carefully into bottles. It is ready to drink, within three days. This recipe is for a light nettle beer. Should a stronger beer be required double the quantity of nettles and sugar and use 1 lb malt extract (450 gm).

Rose Brandy

Fill a quarter-size brandy bottle with freshly gathered rose leaves, pressing them down with a wooden skewer. Fill the bottle with brandy and cork closely. Leave for three months and then use it for flavouring cakes, puddings and custards.

Sherry Wine

4 good-sized potatoes
1 lb (450 gm) wheat (ordinary
wheat grain not wheat flakes)
3 lb (1 kg) sugar
4 pints (2½ litres) cold water

4 pints (2½ litres) warm, not hot,
water
1½ lb (½ kg) raisins
½ oz (15 gm) yeast
Slice toast

Peel and slice the potatoes and put them into a large bowl with the wheat. Dissolve the sugar in the warm water. Pour the cold water over the wheat and potatoes then add the sugared water. Add the raisins. Warm the yeast until creamy, spread on a slice of toast and float on the liquid. Cover and leave in a warm place for two to three weeks, stirring daily.

Strain into a wine jar, insert an air lock and leave to work for a few days or until fermentation has ceased. Bottle and store in a cool place. The wine is ready for drinking in two months.

Vine Prunings Wine

1 gallon (1 kg) grapevine prunings	3 lb (1 kg) sugar
1 gallon (5 litres) boiling water	Yeast

Pour the boiling water on to the vine prunings and cover with a heavy cloth. Leave for five days in a warm place, pushing down the prunings at least once each day so they are covered with water. Strain. Stir the sugar into the liquid until dissolved and add the yeast. Pour into a fermentation jar and insert air lock. Leave until no bubbles can be seen coming into the air lock. Transfer to a cool place for seven days then siphon off the wine from the yeast deposit and store in a sealed jar in a cold dark place for six months. Ensure that the storage jar is full. Siphon off again into bottles which should be corked and wired. Store the bottles in a rack on their sides for another six months before drinking.

I think vine prunings wine is better than that made from the grapes.

When I lived in the Hebrides I used to buy Black Isle oatmeal in half-bolls (70 lb) and the hens and I shared it between us. The flavour of Black Isle oatmeal is unique but when I moved to the Isle of Man and had to look around for another source of supply I was fortunate enough to discover the historic water mill at Sulby, then owned by Mr Brew. It was a pleasure to buy oatmeal from Mr Brew: his family had owned the mill for generations and he knew and loved his work: he knew the farmers and could assess better than anyone the quality of the grain he was asked to grind. Mr Brew epitomized the true Manxman, courteous and kind, unhurried and full of gentle humour. He was never too busy for a chat and when I asked if he would one day show me around his mill he was perfectly happy to oblige me there and then. As he explained the functions of the different machinery his hands caressed the cogs of the huge wooden gear wheels, fashioned from apple wood, he explained, because millers regarded apple as a 'good-natured wood' since it wore smoothly and was self-lubricating.

Now that Sulby Mill has not only changed hands but has to all intents and purpose become a museum rather than a working mill I miss calling on Mr Brew and hearing his varied anecdotes and the simple but soundly based philosophy which he imparted while he was weighing out my insignificant purchase of oatmeal.

I also miss being able to buy fresh oatmeal.

Porridge

There seems to be a misapprehension that porridge made from fresh oatmeal takes a long time to cook. This is not true. Here is my method and it takes only as long as it takes to lay the breakfast table.

2 oz (50 gm) medium oatmeal	Cold water
1 teaspn salt	Boiling water

Put the oatmeal into a pan and mix to a smooth cream with about two-thirds of a cupful of cold water. Have ready a kettle of boiling water and while continuing to stir add approximately one cupful of boiling water. Keep stirring until it comes to the boil again, add the salt then reduce the heat and allow the porridge to simmer for about six to seven minutes. The porridge should now be of the consistency of thick cream. It will thicken as it cooks. If too thick add more water. Serve with top of the milk or single cream, and add sugar only if you must.

Many Bruachites ate porridge for supper as well as for breakfast but even the most habitual porridge eaters were astonished when a woman tourist staying in the village in sisted that all she ever ate was porridge. For breakfast, lunch, tea and supper she desired nothing but a plate of porridge and milk, maintaining that it was appetizing, satisfying and that it provided all the nourishment she needed.

'No wonder she's so pale,' I commented when I heard.

'Aye indeed,' agreed Morag. 'Right enough a plate of porridge and milk is good for one but then so is a potach good for a cow but you wouldn't expect to get calves from it.' I let her observation pass without comment.

'Ach but she's the queer one right enough,' she went on. 'Fancy believin' that stones an' rocks has different sexes like people an' the beasts.'

'Does she believe that?' I demanded incredulously.

'Erchy says she does.'

'Oh, Erchy,' I said dismissively. 'He's probably indulging in a little of his seasonal leg-pulling.'

'That's just what I thought myself till I met her down at the shore the other day just,' Morag responded. 'Me an' Peggy was there gatherin' a bitty dulse an' who should come along but this woman. We stopped for a wee crack with her an' me an' Peggy we just sat ourselves on the nearest boulders but the woman has a good look round before she tries sittin'. She wasn't sat more than a minute before she's up an' away lookin' for another boulder an no sooner has she sat herself down on this one before she's jumpin' up an' rushin' away from it as if it was chasin' her. Peggy an' me we can't think what ails the woman so Peggy asks her straight out if she has a bee in her breeches. "Oh, no," says she, " 'tis just that the first boulder I sat on took a dislike to me and was becoming very offensive." ' Morag mimicked the woman's thin high tones. ' "And when I changed to a more friendly looking boulder I found on sitting down that it was a male. Some males are safe but this one showed signs of becoming very excited so I had to move away from him quickly." '

Morag quite literally wiped the grin from her face with the back of her hand before continuing. 'Says I to her, "How can you tell which is a man stone an' which is a woman stone?" "Most people can't," says she, "but I happen to be one of the very sensitive ones who can." '

I shook my head perplexedly. 'We certainly do get all sorts coming to Bruach,' I murmured.

'Indeed we do,' agreed Morag. 'But if there's any truth in what she says then I'm thinkin' Bruach lassies would be doin' little enough work on the crofts. They'd all be down at the shore seein' could they find a man boulder to sit on.'

Biscuit Pastry

I prefer to use this pastry for sweet pies and flans.

4 oz (100 gm) flour	1 egg yolk
Pinch salt	Squeeze of lemon juice
2 oz (50 gm) butter or margarine	Cold water to mix
1 teaspn sugar	

Sieve the flour and salt together. Rub in the butter. Beat the egg yolk, lemon juice and sugar together in a separate basin. Pour into the flour and mix into a stiff paste adding a little water as required. Work lightly with the hands until smooth. Roll out to shape. Biscuit pastry does not need as hot an oven as other pastries.

Garlic Bread

1–2 cloves garlic	4 oz (100 gm) butter
1 small spoonful salt	1 French or Vienna loaf

Crush the garlic with the salt and cream it evenly into the butter. Cut the loaf into three-quarter-inch (2 cm) thick slices almost down to the bottom crust but not severing the slices completely. Spread each side with the garlic butter and press together. Butter the top and sides of the loaf and wrap in foil. Place on a baking sheet and bake in a moderately hot oven for about ten minutes until the crust is crisp and the bread is heated through.

Alternatively the garlic butter can be made by boiling half a dozen cloves of garlic for about five minutes and then beating them into the butter.

Parsley Bread: Instead of the garlic beat chopped fresh parsley into the butter. Proceed as for garlic bread.

Garlic Cabbage

1 oz (25 gm) dripping or butter   1 cabbage
1 garlic clove, crushed   2 tablespns boiling water

Melt the dripping or butter in a saucepan and fry the crushed garlic clove gently for about two minutes. Stir in the cleaned and shredded cabbage together with the boiling water. Cook for about ten minutes until the cabbage is tender. Serve as an accompaniment to grilled chops or sausages and mashed potatoes.

I like to start my main meal of the day with grapefruit but there are times on chilly winter evenings when a cold 'starter' is not particularly inviting. On those days I like my grapefruit hot and spicy:

Madeira Grapefruit

Grapefruit   Butter
Brown sugar   Rum or brandy
Allspice

Halve the grapefruit and cut round the sections with a grapefruit knife. Spread thinly with softened butter, dust with allspice and sprinkle with brown sugar. Put into a dish cut sides up and bake in a hot oven for about fifteen minutes. Remove from the oven, transfer to individual grapefruit dishes and pour over a little rum or brandy. Serve immediately.

Onion Badjis

2 large onions   Pinch pepper
¼ lb (100 gm) flour   1 egg
Pinch salt   Milk to mix

Peel and slice the onions thinly.
Sieve the flour, salt and pepper together into a basin. Beat the egg lightly and add. Stir in with sufficient milk to make a thick batter. Mix in the onions and form into rough ball shapes by using a draining spoon. Drop into hot deep fat and

keep turning until brown and crisp. Drain on kitchen paper and keep warm until ready to serve.

The badjis are an excellent accompaniment to curries.

Savoury Pies
(to eat with roast mutton)

¼ lb (100 gm) S.R. flour	2 oz (50 gm) suet shredded)
Pinch mixed herbs	1 egg
Salt and pepper	Milk or milk and water to mix

Sieve the flour, salt and pepper together in a basin. Add the suet and mixed herbs. Beat the egg lightly; make a well in the centre of the flour and suet. Stir in the egg and enough milk to make a soft dough. Put into greased patty pans and bake for about twenty minutes in a moderate oven.

Cures – Mild and Drastic

I love collecting old country cures and the following pages contain some of them. I confess to not having used any of them except the soap and sugar ointment (which I find more effective than anything one can buy from a chemist) and the hair tonic which I apply regularly.

A Cure for Asthma

Seven sea urchins: Remove the sea urchins from their shells and take out the stomach bag and intestine. Swallow the remainder of the fish raw and repeat this daily.

Another Cure for Asthma

Onions, sliced thinly and fried in butter until brown then sweetened with brown sugar. To be eaten hot.

Cough Medicine

1 tablespn butter
1 tablespn black treacle

1 tablespn vinegar

Melt together in a pan and take a tablespoonful whenever the cough is bad.

A Cure for a Bad Cough
(drastic)

This cure came from Frank Horne, a Peel fisherman. Here it is, in his own words.

'When any of us kids had a bad cough my father used to go to the gasworks and get some tar. He'd mix the tar in a bucket of hot water and put it under the kitchen table. Then he'd drape a big thick cloth over the table so that it reached down to the floor all the way round like a tent and he'd take whichever of us was coughing by the scruff of the neck and push us underneath, leaving us to cough and choke. We daren't come out until he said so and you should have seen the black catarrh that used to come out of us. But when at last he said we could come out our cough was cured and we'd not get another for years.'

Rough Cider Cold Cure

1 pint (600 ml) rough cider   1 teaspn cinnamon
2 teaspns ground ginger

Put the cider in a pan and bring to the boil. Add the ginger and cinnamon, stirring well. Make sure you are in bed before you take this medicine!

Drawing Ointment
(for festering wounds)

Mix one ounce (25 gm) of soft brown sugar with one ounce (25 gm) of plain household soap which has been softened by being cut into shavings and mixed with a teaspoonful of warm water. Work well together so that you have an ointment consistency. Spread on a piece of lint or clean cloth and bandage on to the wound.

Hair Tonic

2 pints (1¼ litres) water   2 sprigs thyme
1 tablespn grated burdock root   1 cupful (50 gm) of fresh nettles
2 sprigs rosemary (fresh if   (compressed)
  possible)   1 wineglass rum
Small handful fresh sage leaves

Boil the burdock root in one pint (600 ml) water. Cover and leave to stand for about six hours (or overnight). Add one more pint (600 ml) of water and re-boil. Stir in the sage, rosemary, thyme and nettles and simmer until the liquid is reduced by half. Strain. When cool add rum and bottle. Rub into the hair every two or three days.

The next recipe was given to me by one of the travelling tinkers of the Hebrides.

Plantain Poultice

To draw a festering wound gather some plantain leaves and apply the shinier side to the wound. Bandage with a cloth that has been well warmed in front of the fire. To heal the wound once it has been sufficiently 'drawn' gather fresh plantain leaves and apply the rough side of the leaf to the wound. Bandage and leave for forty-eight hours before renewing.

Rose Tonic

Gather one ounce (25 gm) of fresh red rose petals and stir them into a pint of boiling water. Cover and leave to infuse for ten minutes. Strain and sweeten with honey. Drink a wineglassful, cold, every morning.

A Cure for Stomach Ulcers

The roots of bogbean boiled for an hour in water and left to cool. The dose – one wineglass full twice daily.

When my neighbour John was given this remedy by his sister he took one gulp and said, 'Since I was young I have suffered from a bad stomach, even had a perforated ulcer and been rushed to hospital but never have I been in so much distress as I am at this moment,' and so saying he rushed out of the house.

Bogbean is sometimes known as Buckbean.

A Sore-throat Cure

Boil two potatoes in their jackets, cool to a bearable heat. Squeeze them lightly just enough to burst them and stuff them into a woollen sock. Tie round the throat and leave on overnight.

To Bring Down a Temperature

Heat two kippers in a frying pan without fat, cool to a bearable heat. Bandage a kipper on to the sole of each foot and leave for twenty minutes. Repeat in two hours if necessary but it is supposed not to be wise to leave the kippers on the feet for more than twenty minutes at a time.

Wart Cures

Here are two well-recommended wart cures. The first was given to me by Eric Quirk of Castletown in the Isle of Man and the second comes from 'Muffet' Tarrant.

Eric told me that as a boy he once had a terrible crop of warts on the back of one of his hands. The warts resisted all efforts, orthodox or unorthodox, to remove them. At last in desperation he was forced to try a cure recommended by his grandmother who, he says, was always regarded as something of a witch.

She bade him find a snail which he had to put in a jam jar and keep alive, by giving it leaves to feed on. Every day for seven days he had to take out the snail and rub it over his warts, leaving the slime to dry on his hand and not washing it off at all. At the end of seven days he had to take the snail, impale it on a hawthorn bush (it had to be hawthorn!) and leave it there.

Eric followed her instructions implicitly and within a month the obstinate warts had completely disappeared and, he vows, he has never had a wart since.

'Muffet' says she can recall seeing her mother dropping a pearl button into an eggcup full of lemon juice and when the button was dissolved using the liquid to dab the warts until they had completely disappeared. 'They never took long to go,' 'Muffet' swears but she emphasized that it must be a real pearl button – not a plastic imitation.

The fat from a conger eel is good for rheumatism. Just rub on the painful joints.

Comfrey leaf tea is recommended as a cure for rheumatism. Pour two pints (1¼ litres) of boiling water on to two ounces (50 gm) of fresh comfrey leaves. Bring to the boil and simmer for five minutes. Strain, bottle and drink a wineglassful daily.

If using dried comfrey leaves allow two good tablespoonsful.

The powder inside the puffballs is good for healing cuts. Coat the cut with the powder, bandage and leave for a day or two.

Sucking dandelion stems is supposed to be good for people with weak chests. The juice from the stem should be swallowed.

It would seem that in the early years of this century there was among Ladies Guilds, Men's Bowling Clubs, Bands of Hope and suchlike organizations an even more prevalent fashion than there is today for publishing recipe books which could be sold in aid of funds. An elderly friend of mine had a collection of them through which I loved to browse whenever I visited her and when eventually she passed on her collection to me it gave me a taste for acquiring more. In many of these old books the recipes are interspersed with religious quotations, exhortations and adages which, no doubt having been supplied by influential members of the community, had to be included and the apparent indifference of the compilers as to where the quotations were inserted has sometimes caused me a good deal of amusement.

Some of the books include 'fun' recipes like the one taken down by the young lady at the cookery class whose attention was divided between the teacher's instructions and the hat of the lady in front of her. The recipe read something like this. . . . 'Half a pound of blue flour, quarter pound of white

ribbon, half a yard of egg gathered into a bow . . . . etc.'
Then again there were Scripture cakes the ingredients for
which were given by means of quotations from the Bible, i.e.
one pound I Sam. i.24: half a pint of Job x.10 and so on,
and of course there were recipes included for keeping and
cooking husbands!

Index

215

216

217